Shine!
Don't Let Toxic People Extinguish Your Dreams

How to Succeed with the *Abundance with Ease* Solution

(Text and Workbook)

from YourBodySoulandProsperity.com

Tom Marcoux
Executive Coach
Spoken Word Strategist
Speaker-Author of 37 books

A QuickBreakthrough Publishing Edition

Copyright © 2016 Tom Marcoux Media, LLC
ISBN: 0997809809
ISBN-13: 978-0997809800

All rights reserved. No part of this book may be reproduced or transmitted in any form by any means electronic or mechanical, including photocopying, recording or by any information storage and retrieval system without written permission from the publisher.

More copies are available from the publisher with the imprint QuickBreakthrough Publishing. For more information about this book contact: tomsupercoach@gmail.com

This book was developed and written with care. Names and details were modified to respect privacy.

Disclaimer: The author and publisher acknowledge that each person's situation is unique, and that readers have full responsibility to seek consultations with health, financial, spiritual and legal professionals. The author and publisher make no representations or warranties of any kind, and the author and publisher shall not be liable for any special, consequential or exemplary damages resulting, in whole or in part, from the reader's use of, or reliance upon, this material.:

Other Books by Tom Marcoux:
- What the Rich Don't Say About Getting Rich
- Time Management Secrets the Rich Won't Tell You
- Discover Your Enchanted Prosperity
- Emotion-Motion Life Hacks … for More Success and Happiness
- Relax Your Way Networking
- Connect: High Trust Communication for Your Success
- Darkest Secrets of Persuasion and Seduction Masters
- Darkest Secrets of Charisma
- Darkest Secrets of Negotiation Masters
- Darkest Secrets of the Film and TV Industry Every Actor Should Know
- Darkest Secrets of Making a Pitch to the Film and Television Industry
- Darkest Secrets of Film Directing

Praise for *Shine! Don't Let Toxic People Extinguish Your Dreams* and Tom Marcoux:

• "Master Coach Tom Marcoux helps you make new breakthroughs to feel good, get more done, believe in yourself and enjoy each day. Create the success and prosperity you truly want!" – Dr. JoAnn Dahlkoetter, author, *Your Performing Edge* and Coach to CEOs and Olympic Gold Medalists

• "Tom Marcoux has distinguished himself as a coach, speaker and self-help author. His books combine his own philosophy and teachings, as well as those of other success experts, in a highly readable and relatable manner." – Danek S. Kaus, co-author of *Power Persuasion*

Praise for Tom Marcoux's Other Work:

• "Concerned about networking situations? Get *Relax Your Way Networking*. Success is built on high trust relationships. Master Coach Tom Marcoux reveals secrets to increase your influence."
– Greg S. Reid, Author, *Think and Grow Rich Series*

• "In Tom Marcoux's *Now You See Me*, the powerful and easy-to-use ideas can make a big difference in your business and your personal relationships." – Allen Klein, author of *You Can't Ruin My Day*

• "Marcoux's book *10 Seconds to Wealth* focuses on how each of us have divine gifts that we need to understand and use to be our best when the crucial '10 seconds' occur.... He identifies the divine gifts and shares how these gifts can help us create what we want in our lives, and the wealth we want." – Linda Finkle, author of *Finding The Fork In The Road: The Art of Maximizing the Potential of Business Partnerships*

• "In *Darkest Secrets of Persuasion and Seduction Masters: How to Protect Yourself and Turn the Power to Good*, learn useful countermeasures to protect you from being darkly manipulated."
– David Barron, co-author, *Power Persuasion*

• "In *Be Heard and Be Trusted*, Tom's advice on how to remain true to yourself and establish authentic rapport with clients is both insightful and reality based. He [shows how] to establish oneself as a credible expert."
- Arthur P. Ciaramicoli, Ed.D., Ph.D., author *The Curse of the Capable*

• "In *Reduce Clutter, Enlarge Your Life*, Marcoux will help you get rid of the physical and mental clutter occupying precious space in your life. You'll reclaim wasted energy, lower your stress, and find time for new opportunities." – Laura Stack, author of *Execution IS the Strategy*

Visit Tom's blog: www.BeHeardandBeTrusted.com

Tom Marcoux

CONTENTS*

Dedication and Acknowledgments	6
Book One: Don't Let Toxic People Extinguish Your Dreams (The "Toxic Tactics")	7
Book Two: Become Strong and Immune to Toxic People's Attacks	29
The P.O.W.E.R. Strategy	30
How to Say "No" *and* Protect the Relationship	40
Book Three: The *Abundance with Ease* Solution	45
How Ease Unlocks True Wealth	51
Use the Real Secret to More Prosperity	65
When You're Confused about Your Dream … Use the Power of "Motion Brings Clarity"	81
Make the Shift from Scarcity-Consciousness to Abundance-Consciousness	99
Be Fearless, Break into a New Industry and Increase Your Wealth!	125,131
Final Word, Excerpt: *Darkest Secrets of Persuasion and Seduction Masters: How to Protect Yourself...*	142,143
About the Author; Special Offer to Readers of this Book	150,142

* This table includes highlights. This book includes even more material!

DEDICATION AND ACKNOWLEDGEMENTS

This book is dedicated to the terrific book and film consultant, and author Johanna E. Mac Leod. It is also dedicated to the other team members.
Thanks to Barry Adamson II (of MyWordsForSale.com) for editing some sections. Thanks to Johanna E. MacLeod for your editing insights and for rendering
the front cover and back cover.
Thanks to my father, Al Marcoux, for his concern and efforts for me. Thanks to my mother, Sumiyo Marcoux, a kind, generous soul. Thank you to Higher Power. Thanks to our readers, audiences, clients, my graduate/college students and my team members of
Tom Marcoux Media, LLC.
The best to you.

Book One:
Don't Let Toxic People Extinguish Your Dreams

"Two people are slamming me down. One's at work and the other is my own mother," my client Sandra said.

We had an extended discussion. I helped her rehearse ways to interact with the "energy-vampires" and protect her own well-being. The truth is that real toxic people have no interest in change, and they care nothing for your well-being.

In interviewing successful people, I find one characteristic to rise again and again: **Successful people do NOT let toxic people extinguish their dreams.** That is, *successful people have learned to strengthen themselves and use countermeasures to ensure their own success and happiness.*

The strange thing is that close friends and family will often transform into a *temporary toxic person* when you mention your new idea or your next plan. Recently, Nina, one of my friends, told me about her husband's reply to her statement, "I just joined a gym." His response? "How soon will you quit this time?"

Was that helpful? No! Temporarily, her husband had become a toxic person!

However, some people seem to "make a career out of being a toxic person"!

In this book, you'll learn how to use Countermeasures to standard Toxic Tactics that people use to tear you down.

In my work with CEOs, managers, and business owners, I say: "I'm your Executive Coach. I'm *not* your employee. When we're in a session, I'm not your friend afraid to rock a friendship. I'm not a therapist. Some of my clients also work with a therapist. **I'm in the business of *transformation*. I'm not in the business of Band-Aids.** I'm here to support you to *see what you need to see* and do what you need to do to get what YOU want. That's my goal. That's my focus."

So I will NOT ask about your parents and your childhood.

I'll focus on getting you to take empowering action.

The question is what will you do?

We'll use the D.O. Process:

D – deescalate in yourself

O – open up your calm and strength

1. Deescalate in yourself

Where's your power? Where might you have some control?

When a toxic person says something mean and demeaning they watch to see if they "got you." That is, they watch to observe if they have put a dent in your feelings and even your self-esteem.

If you start yelling back, you have given the toxic person what they want: Drama. Still, your actual control is in what you do.

One time, I sat in the kitchen of my parents' home (in a city distant from my own home) and had a pleasant conversation with my mother. Then my father walked up and yelled at me while I was still seated. I saw my mother's face drop in her anticipation of an argument. There were times when my mother would just plaintively cry: "Stop it! Stop it!"

I gave my mother a reassuring pat on her forearm and said, "Don't worry. I'm *not* standing up." I knew that if I rose from my chair, my adrenaline would kick in.

I chose to remain seated. In essence, I deescalated the feelings of pain and anger in myself. My father continued his rant, and when he found no resistance from me—he gave up and went to the restroom.

I was left to enjoy a healthy visit with my mother.

That's the power of deescalating feelings in yourself.

Now it's your turn. What will you DO to deescalate feelings in yourself?

2. Open up your calm and strength

As an Executive Coach and the Spoken Word Strategist, I help clients use strategic action to enhance their success and fulfillment.

In a few days, I am speaking on the topic of "Rise in Persuasion, Stamp on Manipulation and Align with Universal Laws." During the workshop, I will help the attendees learn how to increase their personal strength so they can effectively deal with manipulators and even dark seducers (based on my book, *Darkest Secrets of Persuasion and Seduction Masters: How to Protect Yourself and Turn the Power to Good*).

The solution is: Do things that empower you. I call this acting for your *Golden Tranquility Goals*. Another way to look at this is to support your "being goals." You support your well-being with exercise, quiet time (daily meditation or prayer time), good nutrition, excellent sleep and more. Some of us don't relate to sitting still. So meditative actions can be knitting, assembling a jigsaw puzzle, walking-meditation and more.

When you have developed an abundance of energy and even "reserves"—you have more patience and you can think clearly. For example, I keep a log of my sleep and I change my next day's activities if I get less sleep on a particular night.

Here is the power of developing reserves. Years ago, I worked in a particular bank. My co-worker turned to me as I prepared to leave for the evening. He said some demeaning comments and bolstered his position of working late as: "Some of us have endurance."

Because I had reserves of energy, I did not escalate the conversation. Also, I quieted down any fears that this person would badmouth me to the vice president. I said in a good tone, "I know that you work hard. That means a lot. Thanks. Good night."

Now it's your turn. What can you DO to develop your reserves of energy and calm?

A big part of solutions for dealing with toxic people is to become stronger within yourself.

Toxic people steal energy. Fortify yourself so you have the reserve energy to fulfill your dreams.

Principle: Learn to deescalate inside yourself. Develop your calm and overcome toxic people's attacks.

How will you develop your reserves?

After the above introductory comments related to countering the moves of Toxic People, now we cover, in detail, certain troublesome actions they do. Even better, I'll share *Countermeasures to such Toxic Tactics.* **In Summary...**

Here are just a few of the topics we will cover:
- Book One: Don't Let Toxic People Extinguish Your Dreams
- Book Two: Become Strong and Immune to Toxic People's Attacks
- How to Say "No" AND Protect the Relationship
- The P.O.W.E.R. Strategy
- Book Three: The "Abundance with Ease" Solution
- How Ease Unlocks True Wealth
- Remove Blocks So You Really Succeed!
- When You're Confused about Your Dream … Use the Power of "Motion Brings Clarity"
- Make the Shift from Scarcity-Consciousness to Abundance-Consciousness
- Transcend Fear and Be Fearless
- Break into a New Industry and Increase Your Wealth!

* * * * * *

Toxic People tear others down, and so we will use the mnemonic device of T.E.A.R.

The Toxic Tactics:
T – trigger fear
E – employ criticism
A – abuse (verbal and physical)
R – repeat insults and use guilt

Let's step forward …

Tom Marcoux

Toxic Tactic #1

Trigger Fear

Toxic people like to trigger fear so their victims suffer. Why? It gives them a feeling of power.

How do they trigger fear? They use certain pointed phrases like:
- You should get a regular job. Don't you know that most entrepreneurs go bankrupt?
- Stop doing that. You go to that neighborhood and you'll get beat up.
- What's the matter with you? Don't you know that you don't have the skill to do an advanced job like that? You're not qualified.

What can you do about this? Become skillful about fear. That is, acknowledge that you are feeling fear and then shift to an empowered state of being.

We make the shift by putting into place three different methods:

- Use a *SwitchPhrase*
- Use a Physical Motion and Link it to an Empowering SwitchPhrase
- Rehearse Healthy Actions

1. Use a *SwitchPhrase*

The late Richard Carlson told me something I'll always remember. First, let me set the stage:

Richard was the author of the book, *Don't Sweat the Small Stuff*. He and I appeared as guest experts on a radio show. His friendly smile and kind manner were just what you'd hope a stress management expert would display His energy was peaceful and loving. He knew that I was a number of steps newer in the speaking/author industry than he was. So he took me aside and gave me some valuable techniques and tips. He also said, "It's not that I don't get stressed out. I just don't stay there very long."

This idea tied into something I had written about before meeting Richard. My idea was: **Change the direction of your thoughts by using a *SwitchPhrase*.** By this I mean, pick a phrase that serves as a pivot point for your thinking.

For example, a toxic person plants a fearful thought in you like "You're not qualified for that job. Don't even submit a resume."

You instantly feel the fear rising; you're afraid of being humiliated and being fired if you do get the job.

Then you tell yourself: "I can rehearse. I'll enter the moment strong!" These two sentences combined serve as your *SwitchPhrase*. That is, you step out of fear into a new frame of reference.

2. Use a Physical Motion and Link it to an Empowering SwitchPhrase

My client, Sam, said, "Tom, I get so nervous before I have a meeting with my boss. He's so negative." After an extended discussion, I introduced Sam to the power of belly breathing. I said, "Sam, place your hand on your belly. Take a deep breath. Expand your belly. You feel that motion with your hand on your belly? Now hold your breath for a moment. And then breathe out. Breathe out stress. Breathe in strength. Hold for a moment. Breathe out stress."

Now, before Sam goes into a meeting, he uses the physical motion of deep breathing and expanding his belly. His SwitchPhrase is: "Breathe in strength. Breathe in calm."

3. Rehearse Healthy Actions

Alena, one of my clients, said, "Every day when I take a bus to work, I feel fear in the pit of my stomach."

"What's connected to that?" I asked.

"I'm afraid of what my co-worker George will say. I always feel like I don't reply or what I say is weak. I'm afraid that if my boss overhears our conversation that I'll look weak and not worthy of being promoted."

Alena identified George as a toxic person whom she needed to handle by upgrading her communication skills.

"It's about learning and rehearsing your techniques so they become your new 'default setting,'" I said. "Under stress, we fall back on our 'default setting.'"

I introduced Alena to the pattern "Acknowledge and Add." It sounds like: "George I hear that XY is important to you. And, we can see that 1-2-3 also improves the situation."

I taught Alena the power of saying "and" instead of "but." When she used to say, "but" she was letting George fall into the pattern of becoming more entrenched in his position.

This was one of a number of techniques that I brought to Alena's attention. The real difference arose in having Alena rehearse and rehearse.

"So if you stay ready, you ain't gotta get ready, and that is how I run my life." - Will Smith

I coached Alena through a process I call *Power Rehearsal for Crisis*.

With so much rehearsal, Alena finally realized that she was ready.

By staying positively assertive, Alena faced her interactions with George with her own personal power.

I shared two phrases:
- "I'd rather practice than sit in fear."
- "Feeling fear? Rehearse my dear." [I introduced this comment as if it's a saying by a kind grandmother.]

Toxic Tactic #1: Trigger fear.

Countermeasure: Become skilled about fear and rehearse your "healthy actions."
Principle: Feeling fear? Rehearse, my dear.

When will you rehearse before High Impact Moments in your life? With whom can you rehearse?

_____

_____

_____

Toxic Tactic #2

Employ Criticism

Sometimes, a Toxic Person will use the guise of "constructive criticism" to jab at you. A big problem here is that you want to look professional, mature and strong enough to take "character-building criticism."

Still, you feel beat up inside.

Some Toxic People are sly about how they serve up abuse.

It can be quite manipulative. Toxic People enjoy controlling others.

Here's the solution: You become skillful in analyzing criticism and you empower yourself with well-chosen questions. I first shared this in one of my most popular blog articles at BeHeardandBeTrusted.com:

Move Ahead Successfully Even When You're Criticized

Do you want real success and fulfillment? Then, learn to handle criticism in an empowered manner. The crucial detail when facing criticism is to prepare your own personal and empowering questions.

1. Does this person really want good things for me?
2. What are my personal goals and does this comment strengthen me?
3. Does this comment strengthen my work?
4. Does this comment help me learn and grow?

1. Does this person really want good things for me?

I have an extended family member (a Toxic Person) who has nothing but criticism for me. He's older and he's never been an entrepreneur, author, educator or feature film director. Those are my areas of expertise. However, this person just wants to make me "wrong." Wait a minute! This is a family member, but his goal is "to be right" and "to put the other person down." It's sad really.

When you consider whether criticism has merit, consider the source. If someone is in your target market, that criticism may be useful. However, if someone is merely guessing and has never entered the field you're working in, assess whether to dismiss such criticism.

Talking to my negative extended family member would be **where good ideas go to die.** So I often avoid this person. I have a circle of friends and colleagues who are supportive and still provide me with the constructive feedback that may be hard to hear, but their intention is good things for me. I can trust them.

2. What are my personal goals and does this comment strengthen me?

What are your real goals? Do you want to be famous? Do you want to do good artistic work? Do you want to make lots of money? Do you deeply long to express your creativity?

All of the above have different elements attached to them.

It's important for you to be honest with yourself. What do you really want?

The truth is that I want to serve my readers, audiences, graduate students and clients. So I'm willing to hear tough feedback and learn about areas to improve for my projects. For each book I write, I have at least two editors. They can be really tough and they push me to write in better ways. That's what I really want. I do not want to be coddled.

So even if my editors might occasionally clothe a comment with sarcasm, I still know that their comments actually strengthen me. After writing 37 books [free chapters visible on Amazon.com], I'm a better writer today.

Also, pause and get access to your own intuition. Often, some people are so quick to judge and say, "That won't work." How do they know? And imagine this: If your intuition is correct and you follow your heart—and you succeed—what will they say? They'll merely shrug and mildly reply, "Oh, I guess I was wrong on that one." Do not leave your fate to someone else. Answer your own heart's call.

3. Does this comment strengthen my work?

This is where the real work takes place. A tough comment like "I think that totally fails to engage your target market" may be the best reality check that you need. For example, with a video related to my science fiction franchise TimePulse, my team hit a wall. We needed a paragraph to bridge two sections of the video. I had four people tell me that the paragraph missed the mark. Okay. Back to the drawing board. Eventually, we came up with a solution. With a new approach, we found an appropriate quote to bridge the sections. [See our 1-minute video of science fiction and action, *TimePulse,* when you go to YouTube.com and type in "TimePulse Tom Marcoux."]

4. Does this comment help me learn and grow?

My team members know that I can calmly listen to any comment that points out flaws in a draft of a project. I'll often ask follow-up questions. Why? I'm focused on learning and growing as an artist in the various fields I participate in: speaking, writing, filmmaking and art direction of graphic novels.

My point is that a truly creative person must develop a "thick skin" and also run criticism through a filter. Some critical comments have nothing to do with your goals. Let them flow past like leaves on a stream of water.

Other comments which are given to support you and which strengthen your work may raise your work to world-class level. It's an adventure that is actually worth the pain and effort. It's a road that includes surprising, happy moments.

Principle: Use Empowering Questions to assess if criticism can be useful to you.

Consider some recent criticism lobbed your way. Use these questions:

1. Does this person really want good things for me?

2. What are my personal goals and does this comment strengthen me?

3. Does this comment strengthen my work?

4. Does this comment help me learn and grow?

Toxic Tactic #3

Abuse (verbal and physical)

As a boy, I was terrified about when my father would again throw me into walls. That was not love. That was abuse. Years later, I confronted him about this. I was angry and I said, "Hitting a kid once in anger is one thing. Repeated slamming into walls is evil."

My father's response was: "That didn't happen often."

That's a response of a Toxic Person.

Facing this topic of abuse, we realize that it is critical that *we take strong and healthy action to keep ourselves safe and whole.*

Recently, I gave a presentation and I spoke of how I've taken leadership roles throughout my life. I was hurt as a child, and I do NOT want anyone near me to be victimized. Furthermore, I want to **prevent** falling victim to anyone's violent acts.

When someone abuses you, what are your thoughts? Some people think, "Oh, I deserved that." *NO! You deserve to be respected and to be treated with compassion and kindness.*

Ask yourself: "Is this a **sick** relationship?" By this I mean, is there something that is mentally ill about the other person or your involvement? A brief discussion of codependency arises here. At merriam-webster.com, *codependency* is defined as: "a psychological condition or a relationship in which a person is controlled or manipulated by another who is affected with a pathological condition (as an addiction to alcohol or heroin); broadly: dependence on the needs of or control by another."

My point here is that if you recognize any co-dependent patterns in yourself and your relationships, get professional help.

Here we'll discuss some of the ways to deal with abuse:
- **Get away**
- **Reduce exposure**
- **Power-up Yourself before an encounter.**
- **Get professional help.**
- **Stand up for yourself effectively.**

Abuse is such a vital topic that contact with mental health professionals and in certain cases law enforcement personnel, may be the necessary steps.

Here are some useful ideas in a brief overview format:

1. Get away
Your physical and mental safety are crucial. Make them a priority and GET AWAY from abusive person. If necessary, call upon friends or professionals to help you make the break.

2. Reduce exposure
To state this concisely, **the more you let yourself be exposed to a sick-situation, the more warped YOU can**

become. For example, if you have an abusive parent, and you expose yourself to such abuse too much, you may become physically or mentally ill.

The answer—although you'll likely get a lot of flak—is to reduce your exposure.

3. Power-up Yourself before an encounter.

As my father has aged, he has become bitter and mean toward family members. Before I see him, I make sure to have enough sleep. I also make sure to clear some time in my schedule so I do not arrive already frazzled. When I'm strong and calm, the encounter goes better.

4. Get professional help.

Sometimes issues are so deep that therapy or even appropriate medication are needed. Getting professional help is a sign of strength, integrity and intelligence. Don't let fear of some stigma stop you from improving your own life.

Some useful information:
- The National Domestic Violence Hotline: 1-800-799-SAFE (7233)
- Substance Abuse and Mental Health Services Administration (SAMHSA) National Helpline 1-800-662-HELP (4357)

5. Stand up for yourself effectively.

Amanda, one of my clients, chooses to have her birthday nowhere near her mother. Why? Because is her mother, a true Toxic Person, is a master of cutting Amanda's self-esteem to ribbons.

A classic idea is: *We teach people how to treat us.*

By reserving her own birthday as a day of calm and peace, Amanda is declaring that she chooses where she will be. She also sends a clear message that her mother's mean insults are not tolerated by Amanda on her own birthday.

Will Amanda's mother change? Maybe not. But Amanda's own power will not be diminished.

Toxic Tactic #3: Abuse (verbal and physical)

Countermeasures: Get away – Reduce exposure – Power-up Yourself before an encounter. Get professional help. Stand up for yourself effectively.

Principle: Do not tolerate abuse. Get professional help and empower yourself.

Is someone abusing you? What will you do to keep yourself safe, whole and healthy?

_____

_____

_____

Bonus Idea: Don't Let *Yourself* Become Toxic

In the above section, I wrote: **"The more you let yourself be exposed to a sick-situation, the more warped YOU can become."**

Later in this book, you'll find **21** *Abundance with Ease* **Methods.** They are designed to strengthen you and help you *prevent* personally becoming toxic.

Toxic Tactic #4

Repeat Insults and Use Guilt

"You only come around when it's CONVENIENT to you!" Matilda's mother says with a bitter tone.

"I'm here now, Mom," Matilda responds through gritted teeth.

Matilda has thoughts of "Oh yeah! You want me to come around when it hurts me? Taking extra time off and losing my job? Losing my apartment?"

Trying to convey that information to her mother would do Matilda no good. Why? Her mother does not care. Her mother is only in her cloud of personal upset and pain.

Let's face it. Toxic people are self-absorbed. They often display tunnel vision.

Because you and I are not fully self-absorbed, we can feel guilt when we don't live up to a fantasied-perfect, ideal version of ourselves. The truth is: Guilt is one of the toxic person's sharpest swords. The Toxic Person is happy to remind us of a "perfect, ideal version" that we're supposed to live up to. They use comments like: "Oh, your brother takes better care of me" and "Why can't be like your sister?"

A month ago, I gave a sandwich to a homeless person but still I felt pangs of guilt because I did not stop to talk longer with the person. I had an appointment and so I chose to leave and make sure I still had a cushion of time so I would not be late for my appointment. Still, that self-imposed "perfect, ideal version" was in my mind and the whole situation bothered me.

So let's acknowledge that pangs of guilt are just part of one's daily walk through life.

What can we do?

We make choices based on our values, and we let go of trying to fill a need for approval.

In the example above, Matilda learns to visit her mother — *not* for her mother's appreciation or approval. Matilda visits her mother because that's what Matilda defines as "This is how *I* live *my* life."

Some of Us Live in Fear of an Insult to Our Intelligence

At one of my workshops, Darren, a highly analytical software engineer shared that he was concerned about situations when something goes wrong. The idea was about looking vulnerable in front of co-workers and one's supervisor.

This falls into the realm of a toxic person in some way insulting your intelligence.

While in conversation with Darren, I noted that I've worked with a number of highly intelligent people in Silicon Valley, CA. Many of them have a greatest fear of being seen as stupid and/or unprepared.

During our conversation, I shared what I call *The Pre-Planned Words for Something Going Wrong*. It included two

parts:
1) Preplan what you're going to say.
2) Rehearse your prepared comments.

Here's an example. Darren can say, "These are the three processes that looked vital. So I implemented them. Later, I was surprised by XY. This is what I learned ____."

We cannot protect ourselves from ever making a mistake. However, if we took an intelligent approach to the problem and we can articulate our reasoning, we'll do better in tough conversations.

The ultimate countermeasure to people trying to use guilt is:
1) Have a healthy relationship with yourself
2) Develop some healthy relationships—including friendships

Toxic Tactic #4: Repeat Insults and Use Guilt

Countermeasure: Preplan your responses; rehearse—and develop healthy relationships.

Principle: Some people default to using guilt. Become stronger and let go of the fantasized, ideal version of yourself.

What constitutes a fantasized, ideal version of yourself? How can you let this go?

_____

_____

Summary:

Toxic Tactics and Countermeasures

1. Trigger fear
Countermeasure: Become skillful about fear and rehearse healthy actions.

2. Employ criticism
Countermeasure: Ask yourself empowering questions.

3. Abuse (verbal and physical)
Countermeasures: Get away – Reduce exposure – Power-up Yourself before an encounter. Get professional help. Stand up for yourself effectively.

4. Repeat Insults
Countermeasures: Preplan your responses; rehearse—and develop healthy relationships

Book Two: Become Strong and Immune to Toxic People's Attacks

Picture this. Someone in your life, a toxic person, has slammed an attack upon you. You feel your heart racing. You're truly upset. You wish that you could get some control of the situation—or at least—you want to calm down.

Just reading words won't create the transformation you want.

What's the answer? You need to *Impact Your Subconscious Mind for Your Freedom and Success.*

Why are we concerned about the subconscious mind? That's where Toxic People's attacks do a lot of damage!

Here's a helpful metaphor: The conscious mind is the jockey, and the subconscious mind is the horse. When I was a boy, my father rented horses at a stable in Half Moon Bay, California. His horse got the idea: "I'm returning to the barn. *Now!"* The horse turned, jumped over a small crevasse—

leaving the beach area. I'm 11 years old, shocked as my horse turned to follow. I pulled as hard as I could with my little hands and arms. To my relief, my horse settled down and remained on the path.

Some distance away, my father had to duck his head as his horse raced into the barn. Otherwise, he would have left a "face print" on the barn door frame.

I look at the words "his horse"—and I realize that the horse my father had ridden was *never* "his horse." And we can use this metaphor of "horse as subconscious mind" to our benefit.

You can have an unruly horse and an "unruly subconscious mind" if you fail to repeatedly impact your subconscious mind in deliberate, positive ways.

The power of our subconscious mind affects whether we are resistant to the Toxic Tactics of Toxic People that I detailed earlier in this book.

The truth is: You cannot allow yourself to be swayed in your thinking and feeling by the attacks perpetrated by Toxic People.

Toward empowering you, here are 5 valuable methods:

5 Ways to Impact Your Subconscious Mind for Your Freedom and Success

P – Prove it to yourself
O – Overcome a "stuck story"
W – Win with an Empowered Link
E – Encounter Your Deep Need
R – Replace Inky Water

The P.O.W.E.R. Strategy
Part 1

Prove It to Yourself

You want to feel assertive and in control. Will saying a traditional affirmation: "I feel terrific" accomplish this for you? Sadly, many people report that traditional affirmations simply do NOT work for them.

We need something different and reliable. What is that? Take a small action and *Prove to Yourself* that you are capable.

Being capable is part of the experience of self-esteem. Along these lines—years ago—self-esteem expert Nathaniel Branden wrote:

"Self-esteem is the disposition to experience oneself as being competent to cope with the basic challenges of life and of being worthy of happiness. It is confidence in the efficacy of our mind, in our ability to think. By extension, it is confidence in our ability to learn, make appropriate choices and decisions, and respond effectively to change. It is also the experience that success, achievement, fulfillment—happiness—are right and natural for us. The survival-value of such confidence is obvious; so is the danger when it is missing."

It's suggested by success coaches and researchers that improvements in self-esteem help people have the boost of energy to move forward in life.

In working with thousands of people (over 5,500 graduate students and college students—plus clients and audience members), I've seen that action is what makes the difference.

Just saying an affirmation like: "I'm capable" is not

enough. You need to witness yourself accomplishing something.

People want to see evidence. In fact, in coaching a new speaker I emphasize "A.E.E."—authenticity, evidence, experience. These three elements help one be a great speaker.

So give your subconscious mind *evidence* that you are moving in a positive, empowering direction. Pick something small, schedule it, *do it* and prove to yourself that you are a capable person. **This is evidence that you can use to combat the attacks upon your well-being lobbed upon you by toxic people.**

Principle: You can feel better by picking something and accomplishing it. You prove to yourself that you're moving in a positive direction.

What small action can you choose and accomplish today?

_____

_____

_____

The P.O.W.E.R. Strategy
Part 2

Overcome a "Stuck Story"

"No. That's not me. I can't write. I have dyslexia," my client Clara said. It took a couple of discussions, plans and actions, and Clara released herself from her "stuck story." It was an incremental process. First, I supported her to write a paragraph—then a blog article per week—and finally 52 weeks of blog articles formed most of a book. She now has 5 published books.

Let's look closely at this situation. A big problem with a Stuck Story is that it sounds logical. Clara still has dyslexia. But she now has a team of editors who help her fill in the gaps in the process of her getting her words to her blog visitors.

You can have all kinds of reasons why you're stuck. Still, that's not the most important detail. What is the most important detail? **You're stuck and you want out!**

You overcome a stuck story often by gathering a team or

supporters and taking simple, small steps forward.

A big part of overcoming a stuck story is to transform how you talk about a tough situation.

Here's an example:

Stuck Story Language: "I have dyslexia; I cannot write."

Transformed Language: "I have dyslexia AND I have a lot to say. So I write a rough draft, and my editor polishes the words for me."

Principle: Transform your stuck story by changing the context. Get support and take small steps forward.

Write down your stuck story. Then *Transform* the language. Write about how you're getting support (or how you *can* get support).

_____

_____

_____

_____

The P.O.W.E.R. Strategy
Part 3

Win with an Empowered Link

Years ago, an elderly woman had fallen into a pit of emotional distress and depression. Acclaimed psychiatrist, Milton H. Erickson asked her, "What do you like to do?"

"Raise African violets," She replied. Soon, Erickson had the prescription for the elderly woman. "Raise the African violet plants and give them to people in your church," Erickson urged.

Soon the elderly woman had friends who visited her, and she enjoyed laughter and companionship.

My point in sharing this case history is: This elderly woman shifted in her thoughts and actions.

Her debilitating thoughts may have been: "I'm old. No one cares about me. I don't matter."

A new empowered set of thoughts could include: *"I'm good at raising African violets. I give them to others, and people enjoy them. It's fun having visits with them."*

The above example relates to what I call an *Empowered Link*.

You may have a fearful or depressing thought arise. Still, you can counteract that thought by *linking* an Empowered Thought.

Here are examples:
- I have dyslexia.

Empowered Link: It's proven. Dyslexic people are creative. They make new connections.
- I don't have much time.

Empowered Link: I'm learning to delegate to co-workers and family members. I'm becoming a leader. And I do what's most important to me.

Principle: Don't get stuck with a fearful or depressing thought. Instead, condition yourself to have an Empowered Link to change the direction of your thoughts.

Write down a fearful or depressing thought you have regularly. What Empowered Thought can you link to the debilitating thought? How will you practice your Empowered Link?

_____

_____

_____

The P.O.W.E.R. Strategy
Part 4

Encounter Your Deep Need

I'm a grammar school kid, and Sandy (not her real name—and I do remember her name!) has caught my attention. This is the first female young person in my class that has really caught my romantic interest.

I tell my parents: "I've got to make the first move." My father laughs. That didn't help one bit!

I work up my courage and approach her just as she starts to walk away from the school grounds.

I say, "Can I walk you home?"

"What for?!" she says—total disgust in her tone. These two words, in front of her sister, cut me into emotional ribbons.

I end up running. All the way home. I lose my keys and get in big trouble. I'm forced to trace my steps all the way back to the school. Still, I never found those keys.

What's my Deep Need? To have options! To be able to

think quickly and make great responses. I now call it being prepared for the High Impact Moments of life.

To this day, I read 74 books a year. Also, I practice martial arts moves every day.

The truth is: We need to be ready to respond effectively in the High Impact Moments of our lives.

Currently, in my work as an Executive Coach, my clients tell me that they're surprised how fast my mind works to provide them with options—like a menu of actions they can choose from.

By the way, what could I have said to "what for?" voiced by the unkind, grammar school girl.

I could have said:
- To have an adventure
- To have a new friend
- To satisfy your curiosity
- To see if you'll be in my next short film

* * * * *

Some years ago, I worked with the late Debbie Ford, bestselling author of *The Dark Side of the Light Chasers*.

She coached me during one of her workshops. She said, "When you embrace your shadow you will no longer have to live in fear."

In our conversation, I mentioned, "I'm a leader because I want to make things manifest in the world. Books, graphic novels and feature films."

Further in our conversation, we noticed that I have another reason to be a leader. I have a Deep Need: To not be victimized and to not let someone near me be victimized.

My point is: Your Deep Need is connected to your subconscious mind. You can really empower your life when you face your Deep Need and you become proactive to stay healthy and strong.

So a Toxic Person criticizes you. It hurts. What's your Deep Need? Approval? Safety?

When you know your Deep Need, you can take appropriate action in the moment. You can also take appropriate action to fortify yourself.

I call myself an OptiRealist. I'm optimistic that we can do something and make our lives better. Still, I know we need strategy and effective actions to get things done. And sometimes, you can do everything right and still the thing doesn't work.

Even Walt Disney was prepared for Disneyland to fail. His solution? He originally tied Tinker Bell as the Disneyland mascot because if the park failed, he did not want Mickey Mouse to be associated to the park.

The reason I share this Disney-detail with you is it's realistic that some things go wrong.

Toxic people will try to scare you.

But if you plan ahead (like Walt Disney), you won't be so vulnerable.

Principle: Reflect on what your Deep Need might be. Seek to fortify yourself.

What could your Deep Need be? (A clue is when you overreact to some situation. A hint of what you really need may be present.) How can you nurture yourself to avoid trying to get what you need from a Toxic Person?

When you take care of your Deep Need, you will likely have to say "no" at various times.

Bonus Idea: How to Say "No" AND Protect the Relationship

First, I'll share an example of saying "no" while protecting the relationship:

"Thanks for thinking of me. I know your organization does great work. I'll have to say "no" at this time. My plate is full. Perhaps, I can brainstorm with you right now to see if I know someone who will be a match for the opportunity to address your group."

Notes:
1. As you say "no," you express appreciation and that you know that the person is involved in something of great value.
2. You clearly say "no"—still, you express sadness in your tone of voice.
3. You seek to find a way to be helpful. (One time someone wanted me to participate in conference calls. I was under significant deadlines at the time. I suggested: "After the meeting, how about we have a phone conversation for 10 minutes. Perhaps, I can help you then."

Realize that your first commitment is to keep yourself healthy and calm. If you accept the wrong commitments and you're resentful, you would likely poison the relationship. *Be careful about that.* If you said yes too quickly, you could say something like: "Oh. I double-checked my schedule. I got caught up in your enthusiasm and how great your project is. I have to stay 'no.' I'm sad about this. I do need to keep myself healthy. Perhaps, I can brainstorm with you right now to see if I know someone who will be a match for the opportunity to address your group."

The P.O.W.E.R. Strategy
Part 5

Replace Inky Water

"I just can't get past this. You don't understand. I was addicted to cocaine. I turned my life into a living hell. I was this different person," Arthur, my client, said.

"A different person. That's not you now, right?" I asked.

"Right."

"Okay, imagine your thoughts of the old you—imagine then as ink."

"Okay," Arthur said.

"Now think of this current moment. Imagine it as a clear glass of water. Now when you rerun the old thoughts, you're pouring drops of inky water into the clear water. What do you get?" I asked.

"Dark-tinted water," Arthur said.

"And what do you want?"

"Clear water."

"Yes. So how do you get clear water?" I asked.

"I don't know."

"You keep pouring clear water until the tainted, inky water is flushed out of the glass," I said. "And what are you left with?"

"New clear water."

"Exactly."

A number of times I have used this metaphor during one of my workshops titled *Discover Your Enchanted Prosperity*. I actually do the experiment. I use a shot glass because it takes a lot of water to remove every trace of ink.

My point is that we need to consciously CHOOSE what input we take in.

For example, I recently choose to stop watching a comedy show that emphasized current events. It turns out that to make fun of something, you have to show ridiculous and tragic things. Certainly, I keep up with current events. But I do not need to bludgeon my brain with too much repetition of the latest disasters.

Instead I choose "clear water input." That is, I choose to focus on that which makes me stronger.

I emphasize with audiences: "Ask yourself: Does this strengthen me?"

So the principle of *Replace Inky Water* is: constantly pour in empowering ideas, thoughts and feelings.

Secondly, stop being sloppy about what you're letting yourself take in. Some of us stay glued to CNN and other news broadcasts. Still, an overdose of current events can really deplete our energy.

Life is the dance between what you desire most and what you fear most. That's where people play. – Tony Robbins

In order for you to be strong—even on the subconscious

level—you need to consciously **choose to have "clear water input."** Read, listen and watch material that fills you with hope and new knowledge.

When you're stronger, you won't let Toxic People corner you in fear. Instead, you will focus on doing what's necessary to manifest what you desire most.

Principle: Consciously choose to have "clear water input" into your subconscious mind.

What books, movies, TV shows and music can build you up on the subconscious level?

_____

_____

_____

Book Three:
The *Abundance with Ease* Solution

The essence of being able to withstand the attacks of Toxic People is **becoming stronger within yourself.** It's really about learning a new way to "be" in the world: experiencing and enhancing *Abundance with Ease.*

Recently, I was working with a client, Cynthia, who had just gone through a big disaster at work and her position was eliminated. Cynthia said, "I just don't know what I'm going to do next."

"I hear you," I replied. During an extended conversation, I guided her and invited her to answer these questions:
- What's your gut telling you?
- What's your heart tell you?
- What are you hungry for?
- Where's the fun?
- Who do you want to help?
- How can helping them help you heal a part of yourself?

(This final question relates to doing something that really *resonates* in your being.)

Now it's your turn. Write your answers here:

_____

_____

_____

Abundance with Ease #1

Receive Your Gifts: Abundance with Ease

What if we got it wrong? What if success does NOT have to be so stressful?

As an Executive Coach, I work with people who create Big Success. They push themselves, and they do extraordinary things: Complete and publish a first book, create a company, lead teams, gain visitors (from 173 countries) to their blog and more.

Some time ago, I was about to sit down to work and I felt depleted.

An idea that I've shared with clients arose in my mind: "It's okay to get tired. But let's stay aware. *We CAN avoid burnout.*" I thought about launching a whole new project and product. I took in a breath and felt tired. Really tired.

Then three powerful words arose in my mind:

What about ease?

I've learned that there are times when *our first thought* (like "I'm so tired. I don't see how I can do this") can be misguided.

Shift your thoughts with just three words: **What about ease?**

Think about it.

- *Confidence attracts. Stressed out repels.*
- *Ease attracts. Desperation repels.*

How can you put Ease into your process?

Let's take this to another level: *Abundance with Ease.* This became clear to me some years ago. I took a seminar in which I learned to break a wooden board with my palm-strike. Sure, the breaking of the board represented a "breakthrough."

Then I had a thought. **What if you remove the board?— You could have an EASETHROUGH.**

That's the big, helpful idea! Remove the board or obstacle in your life.

One of my favorite topics that I give speeches on is **"Receive Your Gifts: Abundance with Ease."**

Right at this moment, you have a number of gifts in your life.

Still, the question is: Do you RECEIVE your gifts?

This became clear to me one time. I have a particular elderly relative who is simply miserable. *I gave this person a gift,* and he simply put it aside. He did not open it. *He did not receive the gift.* Why? Because this guy harbors resentments, disappointments, and judgments against a number of family members. He has gifts: he can walk, he has family members, and he is financially okay. But he has *bad habits in his thinking*—so his whole life is full of upset (and metaphorical "wooden boards.").

I see things like this guy's behaviors and his upset-patterns of thought, and *I realize I want a LIFE that is so different from that!*

Don't you?

The essence of "Receive Your Gifts: Abundance with Ease" is in removing the obstacles in this present moment. [Remember: *Remove the wooden board and have an Easethrough.*]

If you only focus on the future, you might live in worry.

If you only focus on the past, you might live in regret.

Really LIVING is found in this present moment.

Is it easy to let go of worry and regret? Probably not at first. Why? We have a lot of "practice" with worry and regret. Worry and regret are connected to three major obstacles. The obstacles—or "wooden boards"—are resistance, judgment and attachment.

Nonresistance, non-judgment, and non-attachment are the three aspects of true freedom and enlightened living.
– Eckhart Tolle

Here I'll provide a few brief comments on the processes of *nonresistance, non-judgment, and non-attachment*:

1. Nonresistance

We lose a lot of energy to resisting things. One of my clients resisted the idea that her mother simply could not be loving. Later, **with nonresistance, she learned to receive the gift** of nurturing and kindness from *her friends.*

2. Non-judgment

Judging things in certain ways can keep us worrying about the future. One of my clients said that he could not take it if he lost his job. In essence, he was judging himself to be incompetent. The positive process was to set aside the idea of "incompetent" and to *focus on improving his skills* both work-related and for keeping himself strong (nutrition, exercise, quiet time…).

3. Non-attachment

When one door closes another door opens; but we so often look so long and so regretfully upon the closed door, that we do not see the ones which open for us. – Alexander Graham Bell

The truth is: loss is coming. The idea of non-attachment is to approach life in a way in which we convert "demands" into "preferences." If we lose something, but we had held it as a "preference," we can more easily recover.

Demands can get us into trouble. We might try to demand that another person love us, or be thoughtful, or be conscious of how their actions affect us. Still, such demands often get another person *to rebel,* and we get exactly what we had hoped to avoid.

Non-attachment is a process of flowing with life as it is. This is opposed to swinging a metaphorical bat of expectations and to try to beat life and other people into submission. Such acts just create misery.

We realize that it can be useful to have a goal and to engage with the process of making it manifest. Still we can *hold the goal with a light grip.* We do what's necessary, but as some disappointments arrive, we are okay because we hold things as "preferences." Sure, an author prefers to have a best-selling book. Still, she is grateful for selling 10,000 copies.

* * *

Let's hold onto the idea of an *Easethrough*. That's when you remove the wooden boards of resistance, judgment and attachment.

Now it's your turn. What wooden boards (obstacles) are in your life? How can you shift your approach to one of nonresistance, non-judgment and non-attachment?

Then you can truly *Receive Your Gifts*.

Principle: Remove an obstacle and then enjoy an Easethrough.

What obstacles can you get out of your way? How can you increase your ease?

_____

_____

_____

Abundance with Ease #2

How Ease Unlocks True Wealth

Years ago, I turned to my sweetheart and said, "I'm running all the time. I feel like a racehorse."

"Run in better races," she replied.

How profound, I thought. It was about being selective. If I naturally like to do a variety of things, I could pick better activities to do.

How about you? Are you running in the wrong races for you?

On some level, racehorses like to run.

How about fish? They naturally swim.

"Everybody is a genius. But if you judge a fish by its ability to climb a tree, it will live its whole life believing that it is stupid."
– attributed to Albert Einstein

Imagine that your natural state of being is gratitude, inner peace and ... Abundance.

Many of us are looking for a breakthrough to more income and happiness.

Some time ago, I had the thought rise up: I want an Easethrough.

Years ago, I attended a seminar and they guided us in how to break a wooden board.

Later, I thought, "Hey, how about getting obstacles *out of the way?* Just move the board out of the way."

This ties in with my idea of ease. One does not need to work harder if one actually has a *Leap-Up Idea* arise from one's intuition. We'll talk more about a Leap-Up Idea in the first part of the E.A.S.E. process:

E – expand to Leap-Up Ideas
A – act on the right risk
S – select "no" [and droppables]
E – energize to negotiate

1. Expand to Leap-Up Ideas

Your path to increasing your wealth rises to great heights when you get access to your intuition and enjoy the arrival of *Leap-Up Ideas.* A Leap-Up Idea is one that takes your business to a great height. One of my mentors said that it's ideal to divide one's attention as 50% to current cash flow and the other 50% focused on building business assets.

For me, a Leap-Up Idea is the story of *Jack AngelSword*. My team is currently working on the first graphic novel of the first trilogy. I already have 340 pages (rough sketches) for the first trilogy and an outline that takes us through graphic novel #6. These graphic novels will eventually become six feature films. **Do you see how this is a Leap-Up Idea?** One story idea leads to a franchise with potential for action figures, posters, feature films, video games and more.

To get access to Leap-Up Ideas make space for your intuition.

Get some time away from people and a hectic schedule each day. It could be simply a 10-minute walk when your mind can wander and wonder.

2. Act on the right risk

Have you heard that to be successful you need to take risks?

Like many things, that's partly true.

Take the right risk and you could leap forward in your career. Take the wrong risk, and it can set you back for days or even a couple of years.

What you need are excellent strategies for *appropriate risk-taking*.

Here is the W.A.T.C.H. process (as in "watch your step"):

- Weigh the benefits
- Align with moral, effective and devoted people
- Take a *360-degree Look*
- Clarify that you won't win each time—but you can take a step up
- Hire the best coaching and advice that you can

a) Weigh the benefits

Is the risk even worth it? For example, when I was in Atlantic City and thinking about whether I would try the Skycoaster ride, I thought about the risks. With this ride you fall 110 feet at 70 miles per hour. Then you do an arc as the cables catch you.

I had heard that some extreme rides might cause eye damage. I studied the situation and saw, because of the arc motion, that it was *highly unlikely* that my retinas would detach. I wouldn't risk my eyes. (That was years ago, my eyes are doing well.)

And the benefit was that it looked like a positive way to "experience flying."

Now, when it comes to deciding which feature film or book project that I'll do—the budget has my attention. There's an old phrase: "Don't bet the farm." I make sure that no one project will overwhelm my company's forward movement.

b) Align with moral, effective and devoted people

Recently, a friend talked to me about how someone caused too much trouble at the beginning of a business alliance. Often, in such a situation, it's helpful to say, "Oh. I see—we don't have a match."

Many times, when you choose your companions well, you may not reach the top profit point you prefer—but **you have formed *good* alliances**. These alliances can serve you well in future projects. Also, it helps to choose moral, learned, wise companions so that you learn good things along the way. Good companions will bring you opportunities in the future.

c) Take a 360-degree Look

What could go wrong? Don't hide from it. Find a way that you can be "okay" if the worst happens.

The 360-degree Look is when you look for:
- what can go right
- what can go wrong
- trustworthy people to advise you
- working with moral, trustworthy, persevering people who are reliable for devoting big efforts to the project.
- your own feelings, wisdom and intuition to advise

you
- ways that you can protect yourself and avoid going upside-down if the project doesn't work out.

At one time, a client came to me with a problem: she felt badly that her project didn't turn out as she (and her team) had hoped.

Through our discussion, she learned to describe the situation in this way:

"We had three goals: make a project that lifted people's hearts, move our careers forward and make some money. We got two out of three. You've got to know that we're going to be careful with the next project!"

Many times, we can only learn by actually *doing the work*.

d) Clarify that you won't win each time—but you can take a step up

I know someone who is a good writer but she won't invest in herself. She won't hire an editor and publish a book.

On the other hand, Steve Alten sold his used car to be able to pay an excellent editor to work on his first novel *MEG*. Thereafter, Steve has published at least 8 other novels, and now has a full-time career as a writer. Now, that selling of the car looks like a good risk—yes?

Did you know that Deepak Chopra, Edgar Allen Poe, and Sigmund Freud all self-published a book? *How is the world going to know what you can do—if you won't stretch yourself to show what you can do?*

You need a big picture viewpoint of your project and how it is part of your career path. For example, writing and publishing a book puts you on a whole different level.

Demonstrate to the world that you *can* do what you want

to do—on a small scale.

I mentioned that "you won't win each time—but you can take a step up." It's true. Not every film, book or audio program I have done has sold to my preferred level of sales. Sometimes, I was just plain disappointed. But I did "step up."

One of my closest friends, a top project manager and text editor who has worked with NASA, the White House and other notable teams, praised my writing about non-attachment, nonjudgment and nonresistance. She said, "Tom, this is your best writing."

You see, writing several projects (books, screenplays, novels, commercials, audio programs) has made me a better writer today. That's having a viewpoint of looking at your whole career path.

In order to write the way I do today, I needed to practice, explore, get scared, stretch, and write some more.

[My sweetheart likes to say, "What? You think Tom came out of the box like this?!"]

My graduate students have told me that they're afraid of failure. I respond, "You won't win every time, but you'll learn and step up—as long as you stay in the game."

e) Hire the best coaching and advice that you can

What can you afford? That's a trick question.

During the Depression, people somehow found the money to go to the movies. It's understandable. People were hurting, and they needed an emotional-resting time.

Have you noticed that people can "afford" what they *really* want?

(Some years ago, I was intrigued about how my sweetheart always found ways to get more yarn and chocolate into the house.)

For years, I consistently ate homemade lunches. Why? Because I wanted my modest amount of money to go to my projects. Yes—I could afford to invest my money in my projects.

About 20 years ago, when I first entered the speaking industry, I invested $200 to hire a coach (a veteran speaker). With what I learned in two hours, I immediately made money at my next speech. That $200 investment has paid for itself many, many times.

$200 was a huge amount for me at the time. In fact, at that time, 20 years ago, I slept in a chair at an airport because I didn't have the budget for a hotel room.

What can you afford? You choose.

Your next step:

Only you can answer these questions when evaluating a risk:
- What is the best result from this risk?
- If this goes wrong, can I still be sure to be "okay"?
- Who can help me—that is, what expert help can I get?
- Have I devoted time and attention to take a *360-degree Look* at this project?

The secret: take time, give yourself space to think, feel and get your intuition involved. Some people make decisions too fast—trying to get away from the pain of being unsettled. Devote the time, space and intuition to your decisions about risks.

Remember and use the above W.A.T.C.H. steps.

Even writing this book was a risk.

I had to do a lot of thinking, feeling and connecting with my intuition to bring it to you.

I'm glad I did.

May your appropriate risks work well!

3. Select "no" [and droppables]

"The difference between successful people and really successful people is that really successful people say no to almost everything."
– Warren Buffett

The truly powerful word is "No." Why? It gives you the ability to do the most useful and beneficial action at any given moment.

"If it's not a 'hell yes,' it's a 'hell no.'"
– attributed to Cheryl Richardson

Some years ago, I had low funds while I was pursuing entrepreneurial projects. On a number of occasions, I'd visit with a friend, Henry. When I'd cover dinner, I would treat Henry to burritos. He told me he liked burritos.
However, I learned later that Henry preferred expensive food. I mentioned, "I need to be careful about my budget because I need to hire contractors to help me get projects done." Ultimately, Henry left my life.
I had said "no" to expensive dinners. It was a good decision for my life. I was saying "Yes!" to my destiny, and I was saying "No!" to using my money on expensive restaurants.
Recently, I did a workshop on my book *Time Management Secrets the Rich Won't Tell You*. Kevin, an audience member, asked, "What can I do? I'm feeling overwhelmed?"
"Often, it's a matter of soul-searching and finding something to drop from your schedule. I call them 'droppables,'" I replied. Picking a droppable can be tough.

To protect my energy, I limit the time I'm around negative relatives. Do I get negative pushback? Certainly! Still, I need to protect myself from those Toxic People who do me harm.

4. Energize to negotiate

To run your own business often calls for negotiating well. How much will you pay contractors? What if you're doing a project that is speculative?

Marc Allen, publisher of the best-selling book *The Power of Now* (by Eckhart Tolle), told me, "In the beginning, we were spending too much to produce the books." The gist of our conversation was that he had to put in controls so that his company was not investing too much money across the board in the books. What does that call for? Negotiation. For example, how much will freelance editors earn in fees? This is a topic of negotiation.

To negotiate well you need to be clear about your Least Acceptable Result (LAR), which is the minimal deal that you will accept. As long as you do better than your LAR, you know you're successful. For example, a speaker whose regular fee is $9,000 may agree to accept $6,000 when she wants to enter a new market. If her LAR was $4,000, then she's still done well.

When you flinch at the first offer, you are likely to get a better result for yourself, and the other person will feel better in the long run. How is this possible?

Here is an example: Trudy considers purchasing a used car that is advertised at $3,000. She offers $1,000. The car owner immediately accepts. Does Trudy feel good?

No. She thinks, (a) "what's wrong with the car?" and (b) "I could have done better." It would have been better for the car owner to flinch at the first offer and express discomfort.

Additionally, take care to know your Maximum

Supportable Position (MSP). Let's say that Amber wants to sell her car and requests $27,000. But a potential buyer looks up the blue book valuation as $15,000. Now, Amber does not have a Maximum Supportable Position. In fact, she looks delusional.

A MSP works well when you can back it up with good reasoning.

I note in my book on negotiation, *Darkest Secrets of Negotiation Masters*, that it truly helps to rehearse before you have a meeting in which you will negotiate.

Realize that many times both people can get what they want—and this is referred to as the "win-win." Buyers often will pay more if they trust the seller, and the whole transaction saves them time and worry.

Principle: To get access to Leap-Up Ideas make space for your intuition. (Even just a 10-minute walk.)

What will you do to make time for your intuition? Will take a walk, knit a project, assemble a jigsaw puzzle, do walking or sitting meditation?

_____

_____

_____

Abundance with Ease #3

Remove Blocks So You Really Succeed!

When you really want to succeed, remove the blocks so you are kind and flexible.

Often success is NOT about overpowering people or situations. Kindness and flexibility can go far in your getting people to cooperate with you.

Be careful about your habitual thoughts. I've noted that our habitual thoughts can constrict our thinking and serve as blocks to our success.

On the other hand, every day I do exercises to keep my neck and back flexible.

I'm looking to be flexible in my thinking, too—so I study a number of books. I get access to various viewpoints and ideas that are new to me. Additionally, I combine ideas in new, creative combinations.

I've learned that ...

Life can place you into a new chapter at any time.

Still, you can declare that you are now beginning a new

chapter of life.

Why is this helpful? You are declaring your flexibility. Over the years, I've learned to adapt when life has tossed in a surprising, tough situation.

One of my favorite quotes is:

"In truth, I am a verb." – Steve Chandler

When you think of yourself as a verb, you are free! Other people may look at their past behavior and give themselves a noun or label like "shy person."

Instead, you can change your behavior. As a child, I acted like a shy kid. As an adult, I take courageous action. Then I'm courageous.

Develop Your Flexibility

One of my clients said, "I don't take vacations."

Then an opportunity arose and my client considered taking a vacation. Upon her decision, I commented: "You are now a person who takes vacations."

"Prosperous, calm, and happy people take vacations," I continued.

Why is taking a vacation a good idea?

It's about refreshing yourself and keeping yourself flexible. You also get access to your intuition, and then you can come up with Leap-Up Ideas that could vastly improve your business.

[By the way, a vacation can be two days. Or you could declare a mini-vacation of "I'm taking the afternoon off."]

Don't block your blessings. Don't let doubt stop you from getting where you want to be. – Jennifer Hudson

Learning to let go should be learned before learning to get. Life should be touched, not strangled. – Ray Bradbury

Remember to cultivate two powerful practices: be kind to yourself and others—and be flexible.

Principle: Be kind to yourself and others—and be flexible.

How can you be kind to yourself? How can you be kind to others? How can you become more flexible?

_____

_____

_____

Abundance with Ease #4

Use the Real Secret to More Prosperity

"What will make a breakthrough for me to have more prosperity?" my client Anne asked.

I introduced her to what I call "On Time Airport Commitments (OTA)."

"People who call themselves average have a form of commitment that they always complete," I said.

"What?" Anne asked.

"They are on time to get on a plane at the airport," I continued.

Getting to the airport on time, for many people, is a "special commitment." A number of individuals will be late for lunch with a friend, but they will be on time to avoid missing their flight.

The truth is: The successful people I've interviewed have more commitments in their personal "OTA Commitments box."

I've noticed that I've put more daily commitments into

my OTA box including: sit-ups, pushups, using a sinus rinse, writing a certain number of words per day and more.

My clients have placed these actions into their OTA Commitments box:
- Walk 10,000 steps per day
- Make 10 marketing phone calls a day (five days a week)
- Thank one's spouse every day for something
- Praise one's girlfriend about something each day

A special note: How do you choose what to be an OTA Commitment? First connect to what you want—deep in your heart. Identify what daily actions will manifest what you want.

As an Executive Coach, I help my clients create more success AND fulfillment. I take them from "cloudy" to clarity. I ask well-selected questions. I often ask "what"-questions and not "why" questions. I've observed that when you ask why, in response the person jumps out of their heart and into their head to deliver an answer that "sounds good."

Instead, I ask:
- What do you really want?
- When you're doing that [action], what will you feel?
- What feels good about that?
- What do you get from that?

Principle: Successful people choose to have significant "On Time Airport Commitments."

What do you really want? What OTA Commitment (daily action) will get that for you?

_____

_____

_____

Abundance with Ease #5

Use the One Step for Big Success

"I long for the big leap upwards to success," my client Muriel said. We talked for a time about what success really means to her. Then I said, "It comes down to one question: Where's the pain, power, and recovery?"

The one step for big success is to engage your full capacities for thoughts, feelings and intuition—by asking yourself "Where's the pain, power and recovery?"

To make a breakthrough, we look at these three vital elements.

1. Pain

Where's the real problem?

My client Amanda told me her mother's mean remarks created a real problem for her.

Amanda and I had a detailed conversation, and I asked questions including:

- Is the pain coming from your expectations?

- Do you expect your mother to change?
- Can you get your support from elsewhere?
- Can you make yourself stronger so you do NOT need her approval?
- Can you learn to shift the direction of your thoughts to something that empowers you in the present moment?

My point here is that often we jump to a conclusion as to what the real problem is.

The truth is: When you truly nurture yourself and shift your habitual thoughts you can often release yourself from "needing someone's approval."

If Amanda realizes (in this particular case) that her mother has no intention of being kind or pleasant, then Amanda can reduce her exposure to her mother's negativity. Further, Amanda starts devoting time to nurture her friendships and to make space to feel her friends' support.

Now it's your turn. What is your real problem? Is it something or someone outside yourself? Is it your own perceptions? (Sometimes, we DO have choices. We just don't like our choices.)

2. Power

Often your power is in your well-chosen action. When you blame someone else for your lack of success or lack of feeling happy, it's a losing pattern. Blame sets up the blamer to feel like a victim.

Instead, see how you can take control of your own actions and responses.

For example, my client Sandra decided to stop waiting for people to offer her roles in film or television. She produced a few short films and placed them on YouTube.com, We learn by doing. In fact, the acclaimed screenwriter-director

Quentin Tarantino discovered his knack for writing dialogue while he was preparing scenes for acting classes. His friends noted that his writing was just as effective as material written for several produced feature films.

Now it's your turn. What small action can you take so you shift away from blaming anyone or anything for your being stuck?

3. Recovery

We can often handle difficult times when we have reserves of energy. Your plan of action is incomplete if you do not schedule times for recovery. For many of us, watching television is not truly refreshing. Taking a walk with a loved one and having a conversation can be uplifting.

I know a couple of elderly people who stay in their homes all day long. They fail to realize that walking outdoors will give them new sights and sounds—and will lift their spirits. As an Executive Coach, I help my clients design their weeks to include times for renewal AND preparation for the High Impact Moments of their lives. (High Impact Moments include giving a presentation; leading a team during a meeting; talking with direct reports or one's supervisor; meeting with someone who could be a great client and more.)

Additionally, consider activities that you can do on your own. These become like foundational pillars that you can rely on each day. Some people will paint, write in a gratitude journal, do some knitting, or even color in a coloring book designed for adults. Meditation or prayer (some quiet-time) can help us feel renewed. A simple walk at lunchtime can do much to refresh us. A 20-minute power-nap can help, too. (Some research suggests that a 60-minute nap is more helpful for one's cognitive memory processing.)

To really rise up and fulfill our potential for success and happiness, we do better when we rotate challenge, activity and recovery.

Principle: Real power is in rotating challenge, activity and recovery.

How will you change your schedule so you rotate challenge, activity and recovery?

_____

_____

_____

Abundance with Ease #6

Your First Thought Can Be Trouble—How to Get to The "Power Thought"

To have more ease in your life and to empower yourself, do NOT remain with your first thought that may be fearful or depressing.

You can *question* that thought:
- Are you looking for struggle?
- Are you looking for trouble?
- What about ease?
- Can you be more selective of how you use your time?
- Does fear have you blind to ease?
- Does fear have you blind to the Abundance-Path?
- What about an Easethrough instead of a breakthrough?

How to Turnaround that First Thought
Set up a pattern so that when a thought comes up, you

don't fall down a negative spiral. *You have a linked Power Thought.*

For example, some years ago, I was visiting my parents. (They live some distance away from me.)

As I went back to my car, I saw my mother waving at me from the window of her home. I had the flash of a thought: Some day she will die, and she won't be at that window. I'm a trained actor (and film director) and I could take that thought and cry on cue.

But I did *not* want to cry at that moment. I told myself, *"I'll cross that bridge when I come to it. I can adapt at that future-time. I celebrate that my mother is still alive today."*

So consciously *Link an Empowering Thought.*

My Empowering thought was "I'll cross that bridge when I come to it."

Here's another example: "I must increase the number of marketing phone calls I make!"

Turnaround that First Thought by Using a Question: "How about making each call more valuable? How? Be more at ease. Be curious. Listen well and make sure the person knows that you're paying close attention and that you care about him or her. Perhaps, the call will go towards a sale or an eventual referral."

Principle: Set an Empowering Thought to follow any debilitating thought.

What is a habitual thought that brings down your energy? What Empowering Thought can you link to that habitual thought?

_____

_____

_____

Abundance with Ease #7

Start with "You ARE Love"

"There's something amazing about people," I said.
"Really?" my friend Adina asked.
"We can take in one idea and then WHOOSH our perspective changes and we feel better!"
"Such as?" Adina asked.
"Here's an empowering idea: You ARE Love."
The power with starting with "You ARE Love" is that you do not have to "find love" to feel okay.

Being desperate for love or someone's approval actually repels people.

Instead, you do that which nurtures you in mind, body and spirit—and you feel better. Additionally, you naturally become more attractive.

"There is no way to happiness, happiness is the way."
– Dr. Wayne Dyer

Start with the premise that you are love—that is, *you are part of Infinite Love—the Source of Intuition*. Some people use different labels like God, Higher Power and others. Express what you prefer. I appreciate the label *Infinite Love*.

This is the opposite of what I experienced at 15 years old. I got the clear understanding that my father could not express unconditional love. He certainly didn't have that type of love for himself. His repeated phrase was (and is): "You do things so that you're not ashamed of yourself."

What? Ashamed? How about you do things because *you're naturally kind, loving, compassionate, courageous, creative—and happy!*

We start truly experiencing Abundance with Ease when we connect with Infinite Love—the Source of Intuition. How? We remove our blockages.

"Your task is not to seek for love, but merely to seek and find all the barriers within yourself that you have built against it."
– Rumi

Some ways to remove blockages:
- Prayer
- Quiet time
- Meditation
- Therapy
- Yoga
- Tai chi
- Petting your cat, dog or other pet
- Dancing
- Walking in nature
- Knitting (or other meditative activities)

Principle: Start from the premise that You ARE Love.

Have you considered that You ARE Love? Are their positive spiritual books/texts that inspire you to connect with a loving Higher Power?

_____

_____

_____

Abundance with Ease #8

When You're Confused about Your Dream … Use the Power of "Motion Brings Clarity"

"I don't even know if I'm on the right path," my client Alex said.

I've seen this a number of times when working with clients who have accomplished a Big Success. I had supported Alex to go from zero, to getting his speeches-material together, to writing and completing a book. Now, with his book selling on Amazon.com, Alex felt confused.

"I want clarity. I want to know where all of this is leading," he said. In answer, I pulled out a sheet of paper. I drew two vertical lines, creating the image of a road leaning toward the left. I drew two more vertical lines, leaning to the right—as another road.

"You want clarity and certainty," I said as I wrote *clarity* and *certainty* on the left-side road.

Then, I pointed to the right-side road. "Still, where the

adventure is ... and the road we seem to be on is this right-side road with motion and discovery," I said, as I wrote *motion* and *discovery* on the right-side road.

My point is that **Motion Brings Clarity.** In the valley, we cannot see our next choices. Then, we get in motion and go up the mountain. Now, new peaks (new choices) are visible.

So if you feel confused about your dream, get in motion. **When you're in motion, new opportunities are drawn to you.**

I had no idea that I'd be an educator, teaching college students and graduate students these recent 16 years. Some years ago, I was directing a feature film, and the father of a young actor on my set suggested I learn about a local film group.

I went to the group's website, learned of Cogswell Polytechnical College and soon began teaching digital filmmaking there. After that I've trained MBA students at Stanford University—two times. I'm currently teaching Comparative Religion on the college level with an online course I wrote for Academy of Art University. I've been teaching comparative religion for more than 14 years.

Remember, Motion Brings Clarity.

On the other hand, Toxic People will criticize you for taking a road that is uncertain. Some will say things like: "Acting? Do you know how few people can make a living with that?"

Wait a minute! Not everything is about money. And how do you know if you do not take action? Perhaps, you'll do a project that makes money or simply *makes your heart sing*.

My friend Jonathan Colton shared this comment with me:

"It's not their life. They're not paying your bills. How much power do you want to give them?"

In the above quote Jonathan is referring to those toxic

people who will cut down your new ideas or your heartfelt dreams. Do NOT release any of your power to them! **Do NOT let them extinguish your dreams.**

Bonus Idea: Communicate Briefly about "Proof"

In my recent *Discover Your Enchanted Prosperity* workshop, I said, "Proof is the fastest time management technique." I continued with, "As I work with CEOs and business owners, I emphasize A.E.E.—authenticity, evidence and experience."

To get people to hire you or buy your product/service, think about telling a brief, powerful story that provides proof of what value you offer.

Recently, I helped a client prepare for job interviews in Silicon Valley, CA.

I shared with her the power of proof as expressed in a brief story.

I coach her to become prepared to tell powerful stories in response to the crucial job interview questions.

(Here are some sample responses below.)

1. What is your strength?

"I provide creative solutions that protect the budget. I was the unit production manager for a modest budget feature film. Susan, the producer, was worried—the production was low on funds near the end of the filming schedule. The scene where the romantic leads meet hadn't been filmed yet.

The scene was to be on a bus. That would be expensive. You need to hire the extras, pay for meals, pay the off-duty police officers, get the permits, rent the bus, block off streets and more.

I suggested a solution. We could build an elevator set in the living room of an apartment I had access to. No need for extras.

Susan, the producer, said, "George, I can always count on you for a creative solution that saves me money."

2. **Tell me about a weakness.**

"I've given this a lot of thought. I used to have trouble with prioritizing. So I took a time management workshop and learned about the 80/20 rule. 80% of your best results comes from 20% of what you do. So every day, at the end of the day, I write a list of the most important things to do for the next day—before I leave my desk. I have "80/20" on my screen—here on my smartphone."

Above, we see the power of story and "proof."
Two additional ideas:
a) Tell your strength-story if the interviewer says, "Tell me about yourself" or "What are you best known for?" (The second question relates directly to your personal brand.)
b) The strength-story fulfills the pattern of P.S.R. (problem, solution, result). When I guided jobseekers during my presentation at the Employment Development Department (in San Francisco), I added "E"—that is, "emotion." The emotional element is: *"Susan, the producer, said, "George, I can always count on you for a creative solution that saves me money."* Susan is happy, and a good emotion makes the story stay in the interviewer's mind.

If you don't know what stories to use in a job interview, try a number of versions and rehearse with trusted friends or a coach. Get in motion.

Principle: Motion Brings Clarity.

How can you get in motion? Have you "risen up the mountain"—and do you see new choices/opportunities?

_____

_____

_____

Abundance with Ease #9

Use the Power to Shift Out of Worry!

"I haven't heard that before. Would you repeat it?" an audience member asked. I answered, "If you're looking for a good romantic partner, you'll do well with someone who is kind and flexible."

To remain flexible, it's helpful to learn how to quiet down worry and fear. When we quiet down worry, we have more options in terms of what we do with our next breath and our next moment. We stay flexible.

I've have worried over these situations:
- girlfriend has a biopsy—is it cancer?
- another loved one has a biopsy—what's going to happen next?
- my mother has three surgeries related to breast cancer
- my sweetheart has a disease that is only solved (after one month in the hospital) by having her spleen removed. (The spleen was destroying her

platelets.)
- I undergo minor surgery—but they still have me unconscious—and they had me sign a waiver (in case something goes wrong on the operating table).

Still, I used something that I learned years ago from the late Richard Carlson, author of *Don't Sweat the Small Stuff*. He told me, "It's not that I don't get stressed out. I just don't stay there very long."

So I've had moments of worry and fear and then I shift my thoughts with: "Until the data is in, I'll act as if it's Good News."

I am not claiming that using an idea to shift out of worry is easy. It's not easy; still, it is useful.

An Example of Using the Mind to Shift Thoughts

Years ago, when I was both directing a feature film and portraying a lead character I had a surprising moment while I was acting in a scene.

Just before filming the scene, my dear girlfriend had stormed off the set. We were in big trouble. Still, I had to go to work. We only had a few days to film with the crew and actors.

In a distraught state of mind, I did my lines and felt a surge of intense, painful feelings. Tears welled up in my eyes. I said, in a voice that sounded like a sob, "Get me a white wall."

My co-producer later told me that crew members thought that I had succumbed to the pressure of directing my first feature film. "He's lost it!"

Still, the crew responded. They got a slab of wood (painted white) to place behind my head. And I did a close-up shot in which my character told a horrible story (this was like a brief monologue).

My mind could shift to big painful feelings (my fatigue and my feeling upset over my girlfriend's storming off the set). And my mind (as the feature film director) could shift to Scene 89. I knew that as an actor I was in the best frame of mind to portray my character telling his extreme experience. As a boatperson, my character saw the death of a mother on the boat bound for the United States of America. In tears, my character says, "We put the mother into the water. Her baby cried. She'd never see her momma again. I had to help..." My character had to help in tossing the mother's body overboard.

My point in relaying this story of filmmaking is to share that our minds CAN shift. My mind could do double-duty as actor and as director.

I'm inviting you to consider the value of flexibility.

On the set of the feature film, I used certain phrases to shift my thoughts.

If you find yourself confronted with a situation where worry arises, you might be able to shift your thoughts for some moments of relief. Perhaps, you can use some phrase like: "Until the data is in, I'll act as if it's Good News."

The point here is: If a biopsy (for example) yields bad news, then, you trust yourself that you'll adapt then—if that time arrives.

Using the phrase "Until the data is in..." is actually a form of kindness to yourself. By the way, if you're not miserable, you'll avoid spreading misery!

I further realized this some years ago. My elderly mother has the habit of waving from her apartment window. I had a flash forward image that someday my mother will not be alive and will not be at that window. If I focus on this, I can get myself to cry on cue.

However, I do NOT want to cry at this moment so I will not fixate on that thought.

And this leads to my closing point in this conversation. Worry is NOT caring. Worry is fixating on an idea.

You and I can care for another person and stay in this moment and stop jumping into a possible, scary future (that's worrying!).

Now it's your turn. What ideas can help you shift from worrying into something that is present-moment focused?

Principle: Worrying is NOT caring. Worry is fixating on an idea.

How can you shift the direction of your thoughts to a present moment focus? (One phrase is: "Until the data is in, I act as if it's good news.")

_____

_____

_____

Abundance with Ease #10

Use a Real Secret of Success that Few Talk About

"What can help me get out of this slump?" my friend Franklin asked.

"Memorize empowering phrases and condition yourself to switch the direction of your thoughts," I replied.

"Isn't that the old idea of using 'affirmations.' I don't like that. They don't work for me," Franklin said.

"I hear you. We all must find things that work for us in the present moment. My point is that I've learned to use a phrase to switch to empowered thinking—to help me make a new, better choice. With better thinking, I actually avoid falling into a valley of no energy and sadness," I continued.

The idea is to choose a phrase to *switch* the direction of your thoughts. [By the way, researchers demonstrate that this is how we purposely create new neural pathways in our brain.]

For example, as an Executive Coach, I've worked with

clients who were stuck. That was their story. I invited them to change their story. Pick a new story.

For example, I was at dinner with a friend and her parents. The person at the cash register failed to type in the father's order of two pieces of fried chicken.

At the table, while we were eating, I saw the oversight and reached into my pocket preparing to get up and order my friend's father the pieces of chicken.

He said, "No. I don't want them. They haven't listened to me three times. No, I'm done eating."

How sad! This older man's story is: "I am a victim. People do not listen to me. I am done."

Even when I offered to make the situation better, this man wanted no correction and no improvement to his victim-story.

What is the opposite of a "victim story"? It's an owner story. It's a story of "I own my own journey. I can devote efforts to make things better. Sometimes I win; sometimes I lose. Still, I can be proud of myself for being assertive and speaking up." Author Steve Chandler calls this "being an owner not a victim."

Part of being an "owner" of your journey is to study how to make your life better. I continually study some of the best wisdom material. Then I boil it down to something that I can memorize.

For example, in some of my speeches, I share my phrase: the "3 i's — Initiate, Inspire, Innovate."

I deliberately chose to place "initiate" before "inspire."

Why? Because I agree with this statement:

Inspiration usually comes during work rather than before it
– Madeleine L'Engle

If I had waited for inspiration, I would not have written 37 books. Instead, I initiate. I just start writing whether inspired or not. Much of the time, as a professional writer, I start writing when I'm "not in the mood."

A few weeks ago, I got stuck. I started three different blog articles. Nothing was good enough. Then I realized that perfectionism was hurting me. I asked myself two questions: 1) Am I telling the truth? and 2) Can this help someone? The answers were "yes"—and I got unstuck, wrote and posted a blog article.

What phrase are you going to memorize so you can shift to empowered thinking? How will you improve your daily life?

Principle: Initiate your action and do not wait for inspiration.

What patterns can you set so you are productive? Will you write (or do a project) at certain times during the day? In a certain chair?

_____

_____

_____

Abundance with Ease #11

Secrets for a Great TED Talk and Beyond —Communicate Powerfully!

"Help me prepare to give a compelling TED Talk," Sharon, a client, asked me. That was the third time in two days that one of my clients asked for this kind of help.

"I have *7 Questions for a Great TED Talk* that will help you zero-in on your unique speech that will energize your audience," I replied. Serving clients as both Executive Coach and Spoken Word Strategist, I formulated ...

7 Questions for a Great TED Talk:
- What have you learned that makes you go "Ooh! Oh, really? Wow!"? (How can you communicate that in a Powerful Story?)
- What is the big thing that, in working with clients, has surprised you?
- What is something that you've done that has unleashed a surprising, hidden power?

- Picture someone you care about. Answer this question: What is it that you absolutely have to communicate to them to make their life better?
- What turned your original thinking upside down?
- What can you save people from?
- What do you know that others do NOT know? And how is that going to serve the listener?

I often work with people transforming themselves to become professional speakers. I bring my over 15 years as a professional speaker, author of 37 books and member of the National Speakers Association to the table. Because I know what it is to be a guest lecturer at Stanford University, I work on my speeches and rehearsals daily.

The essence of giving a great TED Talk or any other speech is that you need to fully commit. Imagine this: How many times have you missed a flight at the airport? Some people say, "I've never missed a flight."

However, how many of us have been late for coffee with a friend? Many of us. Why? Because being on time for coffee is not in the same "commitment box" as being on time for a flight.

I invite you to fully commit, and you begin that process by using the above 7 Questions.

TEDx Talks have been as short as 9 minutes. In that spirit, I'll be brief. I have one more question:

If you know that your next speech is your last speech on this planet, what MUST you express and leave as your legacy?

A Question can take you to great heights of effectiveness and feeling personal fulfillment. Yes, a Question can even open the door for you to feel happy!

Principle: Use powerful questions to focus your speech.

Write your answers to these questions:
- What have you learned that makes you go "Ooh! Oh, really? Wow!"? (How can you communicate that in a Powerful Story?)
- What is the big thing that, in working with clients, has surprised you?
- What is something that you've done that has unleashed a surprising, hidden power?
- Picture someone you care about. Answer this question: What is it that you absolutely have to communicate to them to make their life better?
- What turned your original thinking upside down?
- What can you save people from?
- What do you know that others do NOT know? And how is that going to serve the listener?

_____

_____

_____

Abundance with Ease #12

Make the Shift from Scarcity-Consciousness to Abundance-Consciousness (The Power of Gratitude)

"$50 million dollars! That's obscene for one person," my friend Helen said. She was commenting on Robert Downey, Jr's salary for the feature film, *Marvel's The Avengers.*

We can hope that Robert gives to charity.

Meanwhile, one writer calculated that with the number of viewers of *The Avengers*, Robert earned 25 cents per person. I'd devote 25 cents for the fun and joy his performance in the film gave me!

What is going on with the concern over Robert's salary? Are people thinking that there is not enough "pie to go around?" That's *scarcity-consciousness*. It's filled with fear and the assessment that there's not enough ... and we're all competing over crumbs.

On the other hand, Abundance-Consciousness is an expansive view that the universe is vast and positive possibilities are numerous.

"You never suffer from a money problem; you always suffer from an idea problem." – Robert H. Schuller

Some may view this as a trite comment. However, Robert H. Schuller lived by this phrase. He wanted to make a Crystal Cathedral, and he wrote down a number of ideas (similar to the below pattern).

How to raise $17 million:
- Find 17 people to give $1 million each
- Find 17,000 people to give $1,000 each
- Sell the glass panes for a certain donation.

Robert Schuller did raise the money, and the Crystal Cathedral still stands today. (Some years ago, I enjoyed an amazing show with actresses floating as angels there.)

When you tune into your intuition—which some suggest is a spark of divinity—you have access to lots of ideas.

Imagine—the pie keeps getting bigger. We do not live in a "zero sum game." That is, your prosperity does *not* take away from another person's prosperity.

Here's an example. Before 1995 and the debut of *Toy Story*, there were no computer-animated feature films.

Now, the highest ranked computer-animated feature films include:

Frozen: over $1.2 billion

Minions: over $1.1 billion

My point is: The pie got bigger.

Additionally, many of my former students now work in the computer-animated feature film industry.

No one took anything away from anyone.

Here's the question: *Did someone come up with a new way to serve millions of people?* Yes! Did someone come up with new jobs and hire a lot of people? Yes!

To enjoy *Abundance with Ease,* we need to create a shift away from scarcity-thinking.

The solution is to purposefully make a shift from scarcity-consciousness to abundance-consciousness.

Let's look at the difference:

Scarcity-Consciousness	Abundance-Consciousness
There's not enough.	There's more than enough.
If I win, someone loses.	Together, we can win. There is win-win.
Life is competition.	Life is about collaboration, innovation, creativity and compassion.
No one cares.	I care. I can connect with others who care, too.

"You never change things by fighting the existing reality. To change something, build a new model that makes the existing model obsolete." – R. Buckminster Fuller

For example, one can think of the Tesla car or the Prius.

I invite you to build a new model in your thoughts—an *Abundance with Ease* model.

Shift to Abundance-Consciousness—Use the Power of Gratitude

Gratitude is a strong stance. When I was trained in karate

moves, the instructors guided me to have a strong stance. Such a stance provided support so one could kick. Still, such a stance was flexible so you could move in any direction

Gratitude fills us with positive energy. We can shift to gratitude and step out of a mood of disappointment or even a mood of worry.

To begin the shift, write on a sheet of paper (or in a personal journal), "I am grateful for . . ." Now note 10 things that you appreciate in your life.

Many years ago, I worked as part of tech-group inside a top bank. (In fact, this group accomplished the tech-feat to have the first bank employ online banking. I was there.) This position did not employ my best talents. Still, every morning, I recited my *10 Blessings* as I took a shower. I'd say, "I'm grateful for my sweetheart, my excellent health, my friends, the financial abundance of my job …"

This practice helped me enjoy my present moment AND energized me to even work on my own company after returning from the bank each evening.

Numerous authors have noted the value of starting from gratitude. The universe sends more opportunities to you — and you have *more* to be grateful for.

Principle: Start with gratitude. The universe sends more opportunities to you—and you have *more* to be grateful for.

Write down ten things that you're grateful for. Imagine that your gratitude attracts opportunities you really want. What are those opportunities?

_____

_____

_____

Abundance with Ease #13

Declare a New Chapter of Life

When Frank, a dear friend, killed himself, a new chapter of my life started. A chapter without Frank. I didn't want that to happen. Still, I've noticed that life often pushes us into a new chapter of our journey whether we feel ready or not.

How can we deal well with this? I've learned that there is an empowering stance to take—one of non-attachment. Non-attachment is about holding "preferences" instead of "demands." Trying to demand things or control people just creates misery.

Another way to make the most of our life journey is to **Declare a New Chapter of Life.**

To actually identify something new in your life as a *Turning Point* is quite empowering.

When you declare a new chapter of life, you can focus your energy. You say, "In this new chapter of my life, I protect my time and no longer spend time with people who tear me down."

Use this process. Identify your own distinctions:
In this new chapter…
- I no longer do ____.
- I no longer tolerate ____.
- My new positive habit is ____.

How do we know when to start a new chapter? You get an intuitive feeling. Sometimes, you notice certain "coincidences."

"We often dream about people from whom we receive a letter by the next post. I have ascertained on several occasions that at the moment when the dream occurred the letter was already lying in the post-office of the addressee." — Carl Jung

"…how we explain coincidences depends on how we see the world. Is everything connected, so that events create resonances like ripples across a net? Or do things merely co-occur and we give meaning to these co-occurrences based on our belief system? Lieh-tzu's answer: It's all in how you think." — Liezi

"Coincidence is the word we use when we can't see the levers and pulleys." - Emma Bull

Principle: Pay attention to your intuitive feelings and take charge of your life and declare a new chapter.

Say you *declare this moment as the start* of a new chapter of life, what do you choose to be in this new portion of your journey?

Shine! Don't Let Toxic People Extinguish Your Dreams

_____

_____

Abundance with Ease #14

Enjoy the Best in Life—Use Your Power (the *3 Rs for Effective Risk Taking*)

Do you miss that feeling of joy and anticipation that you had in earlier years? Remember feeling excited about things in your life? You can have that experience again. How? Connect with this idea:
Face risk and disappointment to feel alive!
I have a couple of friends who have a disheartening response to this question: "How are things going?" Their reply: "Same old, same old."
How sad.
Instead, I invite you to consider having a Milestone Binder. You'll take action and try new activities—and then note your experiences in your Milestone Binder.
You note things that you try for the first time.
In my own Milestone Binder, I have these entries (that have taken place over the years):
The First Time . . .

1) directing a feature film
2) auditioning for a commercial
3) performing as lead singer of a band
4) addressing an audience of 719 people
5) teaching MBA students at Stanford University
6) having a face-to-face meeting with a literary agent
7) helmet-diving and walking on the ocean floor.

To put it in few words, I've faced risk often and sometimes I've failed.

I've learned that you need to keep swinging the bat in order to have some home runs.

I've also learned **three important strategies** related to facing risk and disappointment:

3 Rs for Effective Risk Taking

Strategy #1: Reduce the downside
When I do a project, I make sure that the budget is NOT excessive and does not bring down the company. In fact, I have a couple of projects going at one time because I know some projects fail to bring in a preferred income. As a couple of millionaires have said, "You only have to be right 51% of the time."

Strategy #2: Rehearse
Before any first time event, rehearse. In fact, I encourage my clients and graduate students to use this practice: *Any time you feel fear, rehearse.*

Strategy #3: Regroup with a "Celebrate Someone Disagrees" Celebration
I remember when my second book came out. One of my

close friends trashed it. In my mind, I had this thought: "Well, I didn't write it for *you*."

No matter what value you bring with a project, someone is not going to like it. Instead of letting that stop me, I realize that resistance and dislike for any project just happens.

So I invite you to have a *"Celebrate Someone Disagrees" Celebration.*

For example, someone close to me had her book rejected by a committee at a top publishing company. I said, "I'm with you. It hurts. And tell me when you might want to celebrate."

"Celebrate?" she asked.

"Yes, celebrate your courage to put something out into the world. Celebrate your courage and persistence to get something done! And finally celebrate that if you don't put anything into the world then no one will disagree about the value of the project. I call it 'Celebrate Someone Disagrees.'"

My friend got into the swing of things and said, "Sushi! I want to celebrate with sushi!"

Great!

In summary, **to feel those moments of triumph and feeling proud of yourself, you'll need to face risk and disappointment.**

People who succeed face adversity. They keep going. One thing they avoid is the regret of not having taken action.

I do not regret the things I've done, but those I did not do.
— Rory Cochrane

Enjoy the best in life. Face risk and disappointment and *feel alive!*

Principle: To *feel alive!* become skillful with facing risk

and disappointment.

What can you preplan as your "Celebrate Someone Disagrees" Celebration (a book, a dinner, taking a walk)?

_____

_____

_____

Abundance with Ease #15

Take Advantage of a True Secret of Success

"I don't know if I can keep up this pace," my client, Mirna, said.

"I hear you," I began as we continued into a vital conversation.

"Take breaks or be broken," I emphasized.

Skillful plans for Recovery are necessary so you can consistently rise to higher levels of success.

"(Responding to a question about why a number of icons including Michael Jackson, Whitney Houston and Prince died relatively young...) Don't let this [music] business fool you. It looks like a delicate flower on the outside. This is a thorny bush. And to crawl up on that stage every night to do what we love to do, it's not the stage that kills us. It's getting to the stage or maintaining the pressure before you get to the stage. It's the fighting with the money side, the agents side, who's going to take

the money, who's trying to get to the money, who's trying to be next to me. Are you sincere with being around me?"
— Lionel Richie

A True Secret of Success
The top successful people I've interviewed each demonstrated a practice: They skillfully rotated challenge, activity and recovery.

Top peak performance researchers note that during a tennis match, the pro is active about 20 minutes of three hours. The other moments are for recovery and readiness to burst into action. Be sure to get enough rest so you make good decisions! (Bad decisions waste a lot of time when people try to undo some damage that was caused.)

You Will Need to Stand Strong for Your Breaks and Recovery
Just today, my sweetheart wanted me to do a particular chore. I explained that I had just finished writing my 36th book and I need to take a break.

A couple of hours later, I still helped her with her project. So today was not a "complete break." Still, I stood my ground to get some time off today, Sunday.

It's Vital to Discover What Refreshes You.
When you find what helps you feel refreshed, also rotate the activities. My sweetheart rotates knitting, painting and other activities. Why? After a period of time, the activity is not fun, anymore. So you rotate to the next activity. Sleep is important. Still, something active like walking near trees may be just the refreshment you need. By the way, sometimes, alone-time is vital because some friends demand so much attention that walking with that person is like being

their audience—which takes (not gives) energy.

Beware of Family Members' Preferences

As an Executive Coach, I'm able to provide a different form of support that my clients cannot get anywhere else. I am focused on what the client wants to create for his or her life.

However, one's supervisor and one's direct reports all have agendas. Even family members can have this agenda: "Don't Change. Don't Change. Stay convenient to me."

My point is: For you to operate at peak levels, you need to be skillful about your breaks and your recovery.

Why? Because you can become Most Productive when you have access to what I call Leap-Up Ideas from your intuition. A Leap-Up Idea can be something so creative and lucrative that you could even make money while you sleep. Perhaps, you learn how to create a new product—all based on a Leap-Up Idea. Taking a daily walk (with cell phone turned on silent) can give you the time and space to access your intuition.

However, the intuition goes quiet when we fill up all our time with frantic activity.

Get your rest and enjoy when you get sudden flashes of insight.

Principle: True success includes rotating challenge, activity and recovery.

What activities can you add to your daily life that will bring you *both* challenge and recovery?

Abundance with Ease #16

One Step So You'll Feel Better and Expand Your Success

"Is there one action that could make a big difference in my finally breaking out to real success?" my client Veronica asked.

During our conversation, I brought some principles to her attention.

- Act like your own best friend
- Break out of the perfectionism trap
- Answer "What will bring you peace?"

1. Act like your own best friend
"My mother hates my lamb stew," my friend Cindy said.

"Wait a minute. Doesn't your mother simply dislike lamb at all?" I asked.

"Yeah, but–"

"I hear your 'yeah, but.' Would you pause for a moment?" I asked.

"Okay."

"I've heard you do this before. You express things in the manner of 'Cindy's at fault' or 'Cindy's work is not good enough.' To put it in few words, you're not being kind to yourself."

I invite you to be a friend to yourself. What does that entail? Be kind to yourself. Listen to see if you're needlessly berating yourself and—STOP THAT.

Encourage yourself.

Now it's your turn. Are you being a good friend to yourself? Do you take good care of yourself? What can you do to strengthen yourself? How about enough sleep, good nutrition, appropriate exercise—and time away from negative people?

2. Break out of the perfectionism trap

Recently, I started three different blog articles. I didn't feel that they measured up. Then I caught myself and said, "Break out of the perfectionism trap."

It's better to *Set Criteria for Excellence.*

My criteria for excellence includes a) tell the truth and b) express something that can help the reader.

Good. I can do that. Hence, we have this section here.

Now it's your turn. Are your preventing yourself from getting something done because you're caught up in perfectionism? What would you choose to do if you Set Criteria for Excellence?

3. Answer "What will bring you peace?"

At one point, as an Executive Coach, I was working with a client who felt frustrated and surprised that her recent big accomplishment didn't bring the happiness she was expecting.

I said, "Don't hesitate. Tell me right now. What will bring you peace, Serena?"

"I don't know—"

"Don't tell me a story. Just talk," I said.

"Oh. All right. Uh, a walk in trees."

"Trees. Got it."

"Reading. In a hot bath. Kicking back," Serena said.

"Good. Continue."

"Maybe going back to the yoga class."

"Continue."

"Knitting?"

"Are you asking me? Or telling me?"

"Knitting."

"In silence? With music?"

"Sometimes in quiet. Sometimes with music," Serena said, now smiling.

"Okay. Send me an email after you've done one of those things in the next three to four hours."

"I like this!" Serena said.

Now it's your turn. What will bring you peace? What will you put in your day planner and actually do?

Remember:
- Act like your own best friend
- Break out of the perfectionism trap
- Answer "What will bring you peace?"

Principle: Ask yourself "What will bring me peace?"— and then take appropriate action.

Write down your answers to "What will bring me peace?"

Abundance with Ease #17

Focus on Green Tranquility Goals— Meditation and "Meditative Practices"

"The great inventions of humankind," I said to my graduate students, "The wheel, the lightbulb and Puffs — you get somewhere, you can see where you're going, and you go in comfort." My graduate students chuckled about the Puffs (tissues) comment. I think about great inventions and how each person can contribute something great to the world. Just being kind to someone today IS great. About greatness: *There's something that only you can bring to this world. What is it?*

Discovering your greatness includes something more. Endurance and persistence. We often grow into our greatness over a span of years. That means we need to endure the process and show persistence in the face of resistance.

I've noticed that people often miss a vital part of the process: Recovery and renewal.

Once I realized the importance of renewal, I changed my approach to goal setting. To place things in context, here are three forms of goals:

Golden "Pull" Goals

These are your "moving toward" goals. Perhaps, you want to fund college for your daughter. Maybe you want to have a lovely house or take joyful vacations around the world. Or maybe you truly want to make a contribution to other people. In essence these goals *pull you forward*. They are attractive and warm.

Dark Boot Goals

These are goals that relate to some type of pain. It's like having a boot hit your rear end. In talking with certain clients, I notice that some are consumed with these goals. Basically, they are trying to "keep my head above water". These are known as "moving away from" goals.

The truth is that many of us (when we absolutely must do something) are motivated by pain. Specifically, the avoidance of pain: like doing taxes paperwork to avoid taxes penalties. Don't try to deny reality. Use this energy, too.

Green Tranquility Goals

These are daily "being" goals, that is, we're talking about living moments each day as a happy, productive individual. Such "goals" (or daily activities) can include enjoying laughter, getting outside near trees, exercising and enjoying quiet time.

I know some people who are caught up in *Golden Pull Goals* and *Dark Boot Goals* and they are *not* enjoying their lives. This is *not* for you. Instead, add Green Tranquility Goals. I refer to "Green" because it's about growing and blossoming. Imagine if you wanted plants to grow in your garden but you denied them daily sun and water. Be sure to provide enjoyable moments to yourself each day. It doesn't take a lot of time. Fifteen or twenty minutes on a daily basis will brighten your life.

For over 15 years, I have taught college level Comparative Religion, and many students lament that they just cannot sit still for "sitting meditation." I reply that one can do meditative practices of "walking meditation," knitting and more. My own practice is to assemble a jigsaw puzzle while listening to refreshing music.

Take good care of yourself and come up you're your own Green Tranquility Goals.

Principle: Nurture yourself and experience renewal through Green Tranquility Goals.

What will you include in your daily life that will bring you feelings of refreshment and renewal?

_____

_____

_____

Abundance with Ease #18

Transcend Fear and Be Fearless

The guy hit me in the chest with his Ford F-150 truck. In the next moments, I was hanging onto the hood of the truck—my feet off the street. It was after 9 pm, Telegraph Hill neighborhood of San Francisco.

I yelled for help as I felt terror grip my gut.

No one was coming to my rescue. This was the most fear I've felt because I was sure that if I fell off the hood, this guy would run me over. He'd already struck me in the chest.

How did I get in this mess? Moments before, this guy had tried to flee the scene after smashing my sweetheart's truck. I ran down the street straight to the scene. Why? Because the truck actually belonged to my sweetheart's parents. I was concerned that she would slammed with emotional pain. Her parents would get distraught over the damage and no way to recover costs.

So I was moved by love—but I didn't know I'd risk my life.

I know the feeling of real fear.

How is your experience of fear?

Do you let it shut you down?

Every year, I experience some fear because I'm constantly growing and doing new things for the first time.

I keep a Milestones Binder to record my new experiences—and how I pressed forward even when feeling fear.

I'm talking about a *healthy fear*. By this I mean, if I fear how a book will turn out, I'll take steps to make sure that my team brings excellence to the project. Sometimes, I say, "Fear keeps you on the mountain. You'll prepare. You'll even rehearse for High Impact Moments."

On the other hand, by "unhealthy fear," I'm talking about stepping into a situation that can truly hurt you—like that Ford F-150 truck striking me in the chest. I did go to the Emergency Room, and I was fortunate to have only suffered significant bruising.

When it comes to fear and living a life of abundance…

How to Be Fearless

The answer is: Shift your thoughts so **you fear less.** That is, you spend less time in a fearful state of being. Richard Carlson, the late author of *Don't Sweat the Small Stuff*, told me, "It's not that I don't feel stressed out. I just spend less time there." So this idea has sent me on a quest to learn to shift my thoughts and feelings so I spend less time in fear.

The solution is: You and I can acknowledge the fear and then shift from being stuck in the fear.

"What are you afraid of, Tom?" my sweetheart asked. Although for a moment, the question bothered me, I realized that this was a useful starting point.

Questions can focus your thoughts and lead to

empowering feelings.

Pick some empowering questions and answer them for yourself. See the list below.

Principle: Use Empowering Questions to shift from a state of paralysis and fear.

Write your answers to:
- What small action can I take to reduce the damage?
- What small action can I take that can protect me and others from ____?
- How can I nurture myself while doing this project?
- Who can (and wants to) give me some kind support?

_____

_____

_____

Tom Marcoux

Abundance with Ease #19

Release Your Perception of Suffering

A Buddhist idea is: "Life is suffering."
Certainly, we, as human beings, experience suffering.
Still, *is* life suffering?
Do we suffer every minute of the day? About a year ago, I severely strained my back. The pain was excruciating.
Then I noticed something. I'd have a couple of minutes of reduced pain. Perhaps, I was lying on my side or standing up. Getting up from a chair was when the pain hit me like a mule's kick in the back.
So I was not suffering from pain every minute of the day.
The classic comment is:
"Pain is inevitable. Suffering is optional."
– attributed to Haruki Murakami
Instead of "life is suffering," we might note that some pain is inevitable. Still, *we might be able to reduce the amount of mental anguish as we use certain disciplined thought patterns.*
For example, I do *not* say, "I'm having a bad day." Even

on the day when I had to drop everything and rush to my mother's side, I avoided the label, "bad day." She had suddenly taken ill and landed in the hospital. It was not a "bad day." It was a good day with some rough moments. I was able to comfort my mother and even, with humor, bring a smile to her face.

In my book *Time Management Secrets the Rich Won't Tell You*, I wrote that **"you can be grateful and uncomfortable at the same time."** As I typed those words, I felt significant pain from a broken tooth. Still, I was *grateful* to be writing a book.

What if our real heritage is not "life is suffering"? Instead consider what we find in this quote:

"You deserve far more than you have been settling for. Rather than hardship, you are heir to boundless love, forgiveness, prosperity, and healing." - Alan Cohen

I do not deny the existence of pain. At this moment, I just thought of my dear friend who committed suicide. I had a pang of real pain. Still, I can shift my thoughts to *gratitude* for the good times we shared. Sometimes, pain is something we have to ride out.

When I saw the animated film *Inside Out*, I cried. A character experienced real pain. I cried in connection to such pain. Still, I enjoyed the whole film.

Perhaps, the universe invites us to enjoy life as a rollercoaster. Sometimes, you're up; sometimes, you're down. Still, when we're grateful—it's a good ride.

Principle: You can be grateful and uncomfortable at the same time.

Write some things you're grateful for (even if you're experiencing some pain today).

Abundance with Ease #20

Break into a New Industry and Increase Your Wealth!

"What can you do for me?" asked Mary, as she was considering to engage me as her Executive Coach.

"I can hear your frustration. In your gut and your heart, you know you want to grow. You need to grow. And you want to play on the world stage. Do I have that about right?" I replied.

"Yes," she said, her voice trembling as if this was an impossible dream.

"I can help you with that. Specifically, because I've broken into three industries cold. I say 'cold' because I had no contacts before I broke in. The industries were the film industry, speaking/author industry and academia. In that order," I said.

When you want to take your life to a whole new level of success and real fulfillment, you'll likely want to break into a new industry.

We'll use the P.O.P. process. This is being memorable like you want to "pop"—which is an old advertising term about a graphic that jumps forward in your vision.

P – prove it on a small scale
O – organize trust
P – "project-focus" and lead

1. Prove it on a small scale

While in college I won awards for my film and video work. With these accolades, I was able to pull together team members and investors in my first feature film that I wrote, co-produced and directed.

Additionally, to break into the film industry I wrote a screenplay. Let's look at the path of that screenplay in terms of helping my networking efforts.

That screenplay went from one software engineer to another software engineer to a real estate developer to the then-California State Film Commissioner. Ultimately, when I was directing my first feature film, the California State Film Commissioner gained for me San Luis Obispo Airport and an American Eagle airplane—*for free*. This truly enhanced the production value of my small feature film. He said, "Tom, your screenplay has so much heart. I don't see that often."

It's vital to build credibility. Choose to create a small project and demonstrate your skills on the level you're at. Build from there.

2. Organize trust

Breaking into a new industry is about creating trust about you as a person and as a professional. In breaking into the film industry, I created trust by winning awards while still in college. When it came time to raise funds for my first feature film, I had a track record of completing small projects with good quality.

When I began in the speaking industry, I gathered testimonials from people who gained value from my work. Early on, I had this testimonial:

"Using just one of Tom Marcoux's methods, I got more done in 2 weeks than in 6 months." – Jaclyn Freitas, MA

Find ways to demonstrate your skills and trustworthiness—and gather testimonials that cite your good work.

Trust is built on your personal brand. **Your personal brand is the answer to: "What are you best known for?"**

By the way, people appreciate others who have **a sense of humor.**

Just today, I was working with one of my editors, and I said, "What's that smell?" Soon I ad-libbed,

Upon the wind
Upon the breeze
Came an aroma
That displeased

We're still laughing about this.

Actually, I'm making an **important point.**

Are you fun to work with?

Can people trust you to have a good sense of humor during stressful times? The truth is: **Employers tend to hire and keep around those people who are pleasant to work with.**

I support my clients to develop these following facets of their personal brand. I make it memorable with T.H.O.R.: trustworthy, helpful, organized and respectful.

Be careful to Plug Trust Leaks

Recently, I was working with a client, Marva. An entrepreneur, she led contractors by using a conference call. She mentioned her frustration about a team member "Stephan" who slipped deadlines. She would deride Stephan's failures in front of the other team members. I advised that she seek to have the "meeting before the meeting." That is, she would meet with Stephan before the conference call. Why? When she was trying to use "shaming" of Stephan in front of others, she was *losing the trust* of the other team members. Her personal brand would suffer the stain of "ineffective leader."

Using a one-to-one meeting with Stephan and avoiding the process of "shaming Stephan" is part of what I call **"Plug Trust Leaks."**

People are watching. They note how you treat others. They observe if others follow your lead. Take care in how you act toward others.

A Real Secret About Getting People to Trust You

For years, clients, college students and graduate students have come to me to learn to develop their **personal confidence.**

I say, "Confidence is *not* comfort."

It's not about waiting to feel sure before you try something new. When I speak on the elements of confidence, I use the mnemonic device of W.A.K.E.

- Want it from your True Self (not your ego-self)
- Adapt
- Keep learning
- Energize help

The Real Secret of getting people to trust you is embodied in two things: **Do *you* trust you?**—and—**Do you**

tell an effective story.

I'll share an example. Years ago, I learned how to use both the PC and Mac—and several software programs while working temporary positions. Every time I'd arrive in a new office, I'd create a binder, learn a lot and take well-organized notes! I got along so well with people that they would be generous and kind to teach me all about software programs. Do I trust me? YES! **To adapt and get along well with people—and learn a lot and quickly.**

That's part of how I've learned to be a good leader and complete projects.

How about you? Have your organized your habits? How are you with T.H.O.R.?—trustworthy, helpful, organized and respectful.

3. "Project-focus" and lead

People gather around a project. Pick a small project and lead it successfully—and prove to people that you can be trusted.

By the way, years ago one of my mentors said, "When you volunteer for an organization, make sure that you do something you're good at. Don't experiment with your volunteer work—if you're looking for a new job—*because you want to build a great reputation of being skillful.*"

Another part of demonstrating your worth to an industry is to "climb the tree of excellence." By this I mean, you start with people who know you, and you can build upwards from there.

As I wrote 37 books, on numerous occasions I invited guest authors to contribute an article to a book I was writing. I started with local, noted people and then invited additional authors with higher national/world status. The point is the higher profile authors could see that other people in the speaker/author industry *had already trusted me* to place their guest article in my book.

How will you do projects and invite people to team up with you? How will you also seek endorsements?

BONUS IDEAS:

I often work with people who want to "get on the world stage." As an Executive Coach, I help people stay accountable to themselves and express their Highest Self and their Highest Life.

I often provide the following questions to my clients:
1) What are you specifically doing to further your dreams?
2) What are you specifically doing to enjoy some moments each day?
3) What are your recent steps forward that you're feeling good about?
4) What are you in the process of improving or modifying for your better life?
5) What are you in the process of dropping ("droppables") so that you have more space for your better life?

Empowering Questions help us focus our efforts and remove distractions.

Principle: Prove your trustworthiness and effectiveness by completing a project on a small scale.

Write your answers to:
- **What are you specifically doing to further your dreams?**
- **What are you specifically doing to enjoy some**

moments each day?
- What are your recent steps forward that you're feeling good about?
- What are you in the process of improving or modifying for your better life?
- What are you in the process of dropping ("droppables") so that you have more space for your better life?

_____

_____

_____

Abundance with Ease #21

Change Your Starting Point

"You never get beyond scarcity. You have to start beyond it."
– Tony Robbins

The idea of starting beyond scarcity can provide a shift for us to expand our abundance. By this I mean, if we start from a point of view that "scarcity is true," then we might be so demoralized that we do *not* do the required actions to change our current, tough situation.

On the other hand, imagine starting with the point of view of "abundance is natural." Then your brain is looking for details that line up with that starting point. It can be vital to start from the point of *Abundance with Ease*. That is, look for ways that you can remove the blocks in your thinking patterns and daily actions.

"If you believe in scarcity, you don't believe there's anything for you to get. But if you believe in abundance, then you'll go for it

because there's something there to obtain."
– Moonwater SilverClaw

I refer to myself as an OptiRealist in that I am optimistic that we can take action and make our life better. Still, I am realistic that life change requires effort and strategy ... and rehearsal for High Impact Moments.

Sometimes, we work hard and the results can be disappointing. Still, we learn and improve our next actions.

"Success is a lousy teacher. It seduces smart people into thinking they can't lose ... It's fine to celebrate success, but it is more important to heed the lessons of failure ... Your most unhappy customers are your greatest source of learning."
– Bill Gates

Still, I find it valuable to **consciously choose my starting point.** I start with service. How can what I'm doing make another person's life better? How can it help them expand their success and happiness?

Also, I start with the understanding that I enjoy creating things and making progress. I experience happiness in inspiring and leading my team to create exciting entertainment like *Jack AngelSword.*

"Always find time for the things that make you feel happy to be alive." – a meme on Facebook

Also, I start with the idea that compassion is valuable for creating positive, healthy relationships with family, team members and customers.

"If you want other people to be happy, practice compassion. If

you want to be happy, practice compassion." – The Dalai Lama

Finally, if you find that you're starting your day feeling down, see if you can focus on the thought patterns which can empower you.

"We don't understand that the same thing keeps reoccurring until we change the idea." – Bob Proctor

Principle: Change an idea, and you can uplift your spirit. Pick a good, empowering starting point.

What new thoughts would help you to change your starting point?

_____

_____

_____

A FINAL WORD AND SPRINGBOARD TO YOUR DREAMS

Congratulations on your efforts as your worked with the material in this book. To get even more value from this book, take the plans and insights that you created and place them in some form in your calendar or day planner. *Plan and take action.* Return to these pages again and again to reconnect with the material and take your life to higher levels.

The best to you,
Tom

Tom Marcoux
Executive Coach and Spoken Word Strategist

Tom's popular speech topics:
- Shine! Don't Let Toxic People Extinguish Your Dreams
- Connect: The Power of Emotion-Motion Life Hacks
- Relax Your Way Networking
- Power Time Management: The *Secret* Confidence Connection

Special Offer Just for Readers of this Book:

Contact Tom Marcoux at tomsupercoach@gmail.com for special discounts on **coaching**, books, workshops and presentations. Just mention your experience with this book.

==> See an Excerpt from Tom Marcoux's book, *Darkest Secrets of Persuasion and Seduction Masters: How to Protect Yourself and Turn the Power to Good*—on the next page.

Excerpt from
Darkest Secrets of Persuasion and Seduction Masters: How to Protect Yourself and Turn the Power to Good
by Tom Marcoux, Executive Coach – Spoken Word Strategist
Copyright Tom Marcoux

. . . Now, I am in my 40's, with gray in my hair, and for 27 years I have been taking action to protect people.

And now is the time for me to protect you with the Countermeasures I reveal in this book.

Every human being needs to be able to break the trance that a Manipulator creates.

You need to make good decisions so you are safe and you keep growing—and you are not cut down and crippled.

This Darkest Secrets material is so intense that I first released it only with the counterbalance of my most energizing and uplifting books, *Nothing Can Stop You This Year!* and *10 Seconds to Wealth: Master the Moment Using Your Divine Gifts.*

An interviewer asked me: "Who can be the Manipulator?"

A co-worker, a boss, a salesperson, someone you're dating, and someone you think is a friend.

Now is the time—this very minute—for me to write this book to protect you.

I must speak the truth.

These Darkest Secrets of "persuasion masters" are ...

Wait a minute! Let's say it plainly: These are the Darkest Secrets of masters of manipulation. Throughout this book, I will call these people what they are: Manipulators.

Dictionary.com defines "manipulate" as "To influence or manage shrewdly or deviously.... To tamper with or falsify for personal gain."

In this book, we will look on a manipulator as one who deviously influences someone with no concern about that person's well-being, and who causes harm to that person.

Here is the first Darkest Secret:

Darkest Secret #1:
Manipulators Make You Hurt
and Then Offer the Salve.

Manipulators would invite you to go out in the sun for hours and then sell you the salve to soothe your burns. The problem is that we don't notice that this is what they're doing.

For example, you're considering the purchase of a house. A Manipulator asks the question, "So, where would you put your TV?" This question is designed to put you into a trance.

Dictionary.com defines "trance" as "a half-conscious state, seemingly between sleeping and waking, in which ability to function voluntarily may be suspended." Let's condense this: in a trance you may not be able to function freely.

Here is the second Secret:

Darkest Secret #2:
Manipulators Put You into a Trance.

To protect yourself, you must learn to use Countermeasures to Break the Trance.

All the Countermeasures (actions you can take to break the trance) in this book will make you stronger and more capable of protecting yourself.

Now, we'll view the third Secret:

Darkest Secret #3:
Manipulators Care Nothing for You and Human Decency: They'll lie, cheat, and do whatever they need to do so they win—but their charm masks all this.

Let's return to the example of a Manipulator selling you a house. A Manipulator does not pause for an instant to see if you can truly afford the new house. The Manipulator would neglect to mention that you will not only have your mortgage payment of $900. There will be additional costs: home repairs, property tax, water, electricity, homeowner's insurance, and more. The Manipulator only emphasizes what he or she knows you want to hear: "Look! $900 is better than the $1500 you're paying for rent, which is just going down the toilet. And the $900 is an investment."

Let's go back to **Darkest Secret #1:**
Manipulators make you hurt and then offer the salve.

The Manipulator has you feeling good about the solution (salve) and feeling bad about your current life situation.

How? A Manipulator will make you hurt through questions such as:

• What bothers you about paying $1500 a month for rent?

(The Manipulator will use a derisive tone when he says the word *rent*.)

• What is *not* smart about paying rent on someone else's house instead of investing in your own house?

• How do you feel about your children walking in the neighborhood where you live now?

Do you see how these questions are designed to make you hurt enough so that you'll buy?

An interviewer asked me, "Tom, aren't these good arguments for purchasing a house?"

"What we're looking at is the *intention* of the influencer," I replied. "Let's look at our definition of a manipulator as one who deviously influences someone with no concern about that person's well-being, and who causes harm to that person. If the person truly cannot afford the house, he or she will be harmed by buying it. If the manipulator conceals the truth, the manipulator is doing harm. That's the important difference."

Some friends of mine are ethical and helpful real estate agents who truthfully reveal the whole situation and help the purchaser achieve her own goals.

In this book, we are talking about another type of person; that is, unethical Manipulators.

* * *

In any given moment, we need to remember the tactics Manipulators use. We will focus on the word D.A.R.K. so you can remember details easily and protect yourself from Manipulators.

D — Dangle something for nothing
A — Alert to scarcity
R — Reveal the Desperate Hot Button

K — Keep on pushing buttons

1. Dangle Something for Nothing

What do conmen and conwomen do to seize your attention? They make you think you're getting a "steal."

I recently saw a documentary in which a conman on a street in England showed a toy that looked like it was dancing. This fake product was actually dancing because of a hidden, invisible thread. The conman was dangling something for nothing. The Entranced Buyer thought he was getting something worth $20 for only $5. That was the trick. The Entranced Buyer felt that he was getting $15 extra of value for his $5. What the Buyer really got was something worth nothing. Similarly, I know someone who purchased a copy of a Disney movie from a street vendor in San Francisco. She brought the copy home and it was unwatchable—and the street vendor was never seen again.

An old phrase goes, "A conman cannot con someone who is not looking for something for nothing."

How to Protect Yourself from "Dangle Something for Nothing"

Stop! Get on your cell phone and talk through the "deal" with someone you know who thinks clearly. Go home. Think about it. Do some research on the Internet. Listen to your gut feelings. If the salesman or conman is too insistent, get away from that Manipulator. Get quiet. Have a cup of water. Cool down. Break the Trance!

Break the Trance and Identify the Crucial Detail

Earlier, I mentioned that a Manipulator puts you into a trance. An added problem is that we put ourselves into a trance. For example, as you read this, are you thinking about your right toe? Most likely not (unless you stubbed your toe recently). The point is that we only focus on a tiny percentage of what is going on in our life.

Around fifteen years ago, I caused myself trouble because I put myself into a trance. I discovered that under certain conditions, friendship can make you nearly deaf. Here's how: I was producing a song for a motion picture. A good friend was singing backup in the chorus. Because of our friendship, I wanted him to sound great. I completely missed the Crucial Detail. In this kind of situation, the Crucial Detail is that what truly counts is how the lead singer sounds! I made a song that I could not release. What a waste of time and money! I had put myself into a trance.

In any situation in which the Manipulator is "dangling something for nothing," we often fall into a trance and miss the Crucial Detail. The most important detail is *not* that we're saving money if we order before midnight tonight. What counts is whether the product creates a lasting, crucial benefit in our lives. And is the benefit of the product worth the cost? Some people even program themselves to make mistakes by saying, "I can't pass up a bargain." The bargain is *not* the Crucial Detail.

Secrets to Break the Trance

This is the process of B.R.E.A.K.S. It will help you remember the proven methods to break a trance.

B — Breathe
R — Relax
E — Envision
A — Act on aromas
K — Keep moving

S — Smile

Secret #1: Breathe

Remember Secret #1: Manipulators make you hurt and then offer the salve. The Manipulator wants to put you into a state of being that fills you with a sense of urgency and anxiety. Oh, no! I'm going to miss the sale!

Stop this highly vulnerable state. Take a deep breath. Do it now. Take a deep breath and let your belly "get fat" by filling it with air. As you breathe out, let your belly deflate. Breathe in through your nose and breathe out through your mouth. This is called belly-breathing. Repeat the actions of belly-breathing three times. Good. Now, do you feel different? Remember, when you are relaxed, you are strong.

Secret #2: Relax

You become stronger when you condition yourself to relax in the face of adversity. Researchers note that when an Olympic athlete is confronted with the most stressful moment in her life, she has prepared in advance. She has given herself ways to calm down. Two powerful methods are described in this section about B.R.E.A.K.S. One is breathing, and the other is envisioning.

A special part of relaxing is the effective use of your posture ...

End of Excerpt from
Darkest Secrets of Persuasion and Seduction Masters: How to Protect Yourself and Turn the Power to Good

Purchase your copy of this book (paperback or ebook) at Amazon.com or BarnesandNoble.com
See **Free Chapters** of Tom Marcoux's 37 books at http://amzn.to/ZiCTRj

ABOUT THE AUTHOR

You want more and better, right? Imagine fulfilling your Big Dream.

Tom Marcoux can help you—in that he's coached thousands of people: CEOs, small business leaders, graduate students (at Stanford University) speakers, and authors.

Marcoux is known as an effective **Executive Coach** and **Spoken Word Strategist.**

(and Thought Leader—okay, writing 37 books helped with that!)

** *CEOs, Vice-Presidents, Other Executives, Small Business Leaders:*

You know that leading people and speaking at your best can be tough.

Marcoux solves problems while helping you amplify your own Charisma, Confidence and Control of Time.

Interested? Email Marcoux—tomsupercoach@gmail.com

Ask for a *Special Report:*

* 9 Deadly Mistakes to Avoid for Your Next Speech

** *Speakers, Experts—for a great TED Talk, Book, Audio Book, Speeches, YouTube Videos.*

Marcoux solve problems while helping you to make your

Concise, Compelling Message that gets people to trust you and get what you're offering (product, service, *an idea*).

Yes—the *San Francisco Examiner* designated Tom Marcoux as "The Personal Branding Instructor."

Marcoux is an expert on STORY. He won a Special Award at the EMMY AWARDS, and he directed a feature film that went to the CANNES FILM MARKET and earned international distribution.

(Marcoux helps you *be heard and be trusted*—a focus point of his 16th Anniversary edition book, *Connect: High Trust Communication for Your Success in Business and Life*.)

As a CEO, Marcoux leads teams in the United Kingdom, India and the USA. Marcoux guides clients & audiences (IBM, Sun Microsystems, etc.) in leadership, team-building, power time management and branding. See Tom's Popular BLOG: www.TomSuperCoach.com

Specialties: coach to CEOS * Executives * Small Business owners * Leaders * Speakers * Experts * Authors * Academics

One of his *Darkest Secrets* books rose to #1 on Amazon.com Hot New Releases in Business Life (and in Business Communication). A member of the National Speakers Association for over 15 years, he is a professional coach and guest expert on TV, radio, and print.

Marcoux addressed National Association of Broadcasters' Conference six years running. With a degree in psychology, Tom is a guest lecturer at **Stanford University**, DeAnza, & California State University, and teaches business communication, designing careers, public speaking, science fiction cinema/literature and comparative religion at Academy of Art University. He is engaged in book/film projects *Crystal Pegasus* (children's) and *Jack AngelSword* (thriller-fantasy). See Tom's well-received blogs

at www.BeHeardandBeTrusted.com

at www.YourBodySoulandProsperity.com

Consider engaging **Tom Marcoux as your Executive Coach.**

"As Tom's client for many years, I have benefited from his wisdom and strategic approach. Do your career and personal life a big favor and get his books and engage him as **your Executive Coach**." – Dr. JoAnn Dahlkoetter, author of *Your Performing Edge* and Coach to CEOs and Olympic Gold Medalists

"**Tom Marcoux coached me to get more done in 10 days than other coaches in 2 years.**" – Brad Carlson, CEO of MindStrong LLC

As the Spoken Word Strategist, Tom Marcoux can help you with **speech writing** and **coaching for your best performance.**

As Tom says, *Make Your Speech a Pleasant Beach.*

Join Tom's Linkedin.com group: *Executive Public Speaking and Communication Power.*

At Google+: join the community "Create Your Best Life – Charisma & Confidence"

Get a **Free** report: "9 Deadly Mistakes to Avoid for Your Next Speech and 9 Surefire Methods" at http://tomsupercoach.com/freereport9Mistakes4Speech.html

Tom Marcoux has trained CEOs, small business owners, and graduate students to speak with impact and gain audiences' tremendous approval and cooperation. *Learn how to present and get thunderous applause!*

"Tom, Thanks for your coaching and work with me on revising my speech at a major university. Working with you has been so enlightening for me. Through your gentle prodding and guidance, I was able to write a speech that connects with the audience. I wish everyone could experience the transformation I have undergone. You have helped me discover the warm and compelling stories that now make my speech reach hearts and uplift minds. This was truly an empowering experience. I cannot thank you enough for your great assistance." — J.S.

"Tom Marcoux has been an NAB Conference favorite [speaker] for six years. And he is very energetic."

– John Marino, Vice President, National Association of Broadcasters, Washington, D.C.

"Using just one of Tom Marcoux's methods, I got more done in 2 weeks than in 6 months."

– Jaclyn Freitas, M.A.

Tom's popular speech topics:
- Shine! Don't Let Toxic People Extinguish Your Dreams
- Connect: The Power of Emotion-Motion Life Hacks
- Relax Your Way Networking
- Power Time Management: The *Secret* Confidence Connection

Tom's Coaching features innovations:
- Dynamic Rehearsal
- Power Rehearsal for Crisis
- The Charisma Advantage that Saves You Time

Become a fan of Tom's graphic novels/feature films:
- Fantasy Thriller: *Jack AngelSword*
  type "JackAngelSword" at Facebook.com
- Science fiction: *TimePulse*
  www.facebook.com/timepulsegraphicnovel
- Children's Fantasy: *Crystal Pegasus*
  www.facebook.com/crystalpegasusandrose

See **Free Chapters** of Tom Marcoux's 37 books at http://amzn.to/ZiCTRj   Amazon.com

Your Notes:

_____

_____

_____

_____

_____

_____

Area for Your Sketches of Your Ideas:

www.ingramcontent.com/pod-product-compliance
Lightning Source LLC
Chambersburg PA
CBHW070455100426
42743CB00010B/1632